Reader Reviews

S antosh Nambiar's *The Art of Conscious Balance* shows us that the experience of adversity can serve as a catalyst for personal transformation. By taking us through his life journey he awakens us to the depth of meaning that is possible to achieve in life when we develop more awareness, presence and mindfulness.

Dr Rakshinda Kabir, Monash University Australia.

Mind & Body wellness expert.

* * *

Santosh's book is a journey for the senses. Evocatively, beautifully written it transports you to the world he has inhabited and thence to the simplicity and power of his message. For anyone seeking to more deeply understand their journey or find more peace I would recommend joining Santosh as he takes you into his world.

Tara Garson Flower, Head of Customer Solution Management Amazon Web Services (AWS)

* * *

In this book, Santosh courageously and candidly reveals his own shortcomings and growing pains, and how these inferiorities help him transform. After an arduous soul searching, he went from a mind-dominated individual to a conscious being, similar to the breakthrough of a beautiful butterfly from a cocooned caterpillar. What he left behind was a hard shell of ignorance and self-identification. His journey of transformation resonates with and assures me that I am not alone with my quest for meaning in life. I feel inspired by Santosh's story, and I am confident that other readers will be inspired too.

Khamseng Sengsouvanh,

Melbourne

*   *   *

I am inspired by Santosh's courage and honesty in sharing his life's journey in this book.

His ability to share his stories and invite readers to reflect on the lessons learnt is powerful and effective.

This book presents an opportunity to draw on his wisdom around the art of mindfulness and how we each have a choice to live a joyful and abundant life.

Debbie Lee, Multicultural Business ministerial Council Member — Victorian Government.

Deloitte- Australia, Senior consultant.

*   *   *

In this book, Santosh Nambiar outlines his journey from a village in Kerala to a mindful global citizen. It is a raw, authentic, thought provoking and uplifting narrative for the soul. His lessons provide a blueprint on how to transform ourselves which in turn produces miracles for those around us.

Dr Tom Verghese

Speaker, Author, cross cultural consultant and executive coach, founder cultural synergies.

* * *

This is a story of a small-town boy whose life takes him through an emotional rollercoaster only to come to realise his true self hidden beneath the layers of the conditioned self. It is about finding your own path, your own rhythm towards a well-balanced, grounded and conscious life. The author has beautifully shared his inner journey and how he was able to realize the full potential of the intellect vs intelligence and summarised it as — the 'art of conscious balance' for the Six Cs of life.

If we forget who we are right now and get into the spirit of this little boy as we read this story, what we will experience, will indeed be our personal reflection, of who perhaps we are with all our struggles in life and who we can be if we are able to realise this simple truth of life.

Ravi Ram Mohan, Multi Domain expert in Green Energy Initiatives — Healthcare and Aerospace

* * *

This gentle autobiographical tale has a real sting in its tail, a strong message for those of us who enjoy a good read with some meaty substance. Santosh paints a beautiful picture of an idyllic childhood in a small village in Southern India. A perfect backdrop and loving foundation for a life which from most perspectives would appear fulfilled, but which threatens to unravel when crisis appears. And as often happens, a crisis is exactly what may be needed to wake us up from the deeply conditioned way of living. To me, this is the real substance of this delightful book, the insights Santosh realises through his own investigations and eloquently shares, will be a help and inspiration for all seekers of truth (and those who do not yet know they are on a seeking path).

I am greatly appreciative of Santosh's (and others) efforts in bringing such a message of hope through the telling of their journey to awakening, there is much to share and many thirsty travellers.

Glenn Grayston — Auckland University of Technology. Auckland.

* * *

A book that will appeal strongly to any thinking person, particularly a seeker. As an educator, I found this exploration of Santosh Nambiar quite remarkable in many ways. Most importantly, I was struck by how he relied on his Inner Teacher to find answers to deep questions that have plagued humankind since time immemorial. And I am left asking, as he does: Why don't schools talk about this? A very inspiring read ...!

Dr. Neeraja Raghavan (Princeton University)

Founder Director, Thinking Teacher

*   *   *

Santosh's book is a fascinating account of the transformational journey of his life so far. Santosh shares with us the challenges life threw at him at various points on this journey and how these experiences forced him to self-introspect and try to understand the very purpose of it all. He has found peace and a meaning to his life through this process of introspection. I would strongly recommend this book to anyone who has the inclination to pause and undertake a self-examination.

Anil Nair, Senior executive Engineer, Metro trains

Melbourne, Australia

*   *   *

Santhosh Nambiar's book on his inner journey or rather his amazing journey from his picturesque village in Kerala, to his life in New Zealand and Australia is a must read.

Prof. Murali Naidu

Professor — Neuroscience, University of Malay, Malaysia

*   *   *

Easy to read and understand the difference between Intellect and Intelligence.

In his latest book *The Art of Conscious Balance* Santosh Nambiar makes readers aware of the difference between the intellect and intelligence. How limited and constrained one's intellect is and how one can open up to the vastness (unlimited) of the intelligence in the universe, that would open up a path to peace, joy and happiness in one's life. Great read and presented in an easy-to-understand format by the author. I highly recommend this book.

Prof. Adrian Perrig Professor at ETH Zurich,

Co-Founder Anapaya Systems, , Zurich, Switzerland

*   *   *

A wonderful read! Santosh gives sage advice about following the intelligence of the universe vs. relying on your own (comparatively) small intellect. I would recommend this book to anyone looking to understand themselves better - for those yearning for guidance and light from someone who truly knows and understands.

Joe Keller, Author Nevada USA.

*   *   *

This book is a strong call to understand self and gain a better understanding of human behaviour. The questions Santosh has asked in the book will shake the foundations of the mind conceived conditioned self and will set you on a path to explore the true self — who you truly are. Well written and refreshing to read.

Sue Block, Melbourne

*   *   *

This is a refreshing and easy to read story of the author's personal journey through life. Yet it is both powerful and insightful. Santosh is brutally honest about his character and experiences, which allow the reader to discover or, perhaps rediscover, a deep understanding of their own insecurities and selfishness. Importantly, Santosh provides a way to how we can all become better human beings by understanding, and striving for, aConscious Balance.

Dr Ian Beckman, Senior Scientist

(Husband, Father and Grandfather)

College of Medicine and Public Health

Flinders University, South Australia

Department of Vascular and Endovascular Surgery

Flinders Medical Centre, Australia.

*   *   *

Put this book, *The Art of Conscious Balance* **, by author Santosh Nambiar,** **on your must read list for the New Year, 2022.**

I was absorbed by the gentle sympathetic writing and the question posed in this book, "Why do we spend our time struggling and dissatisfied when our existence on earth is so short?" Through real life situations and life stories, Santosh shows us how to respond better to the constant chatter in your brain. He had measured his life against a random comment from childhood — that he was "good for nothing", and his driving force had been to prove this wrong and erase it from his brain.

He found that the answer to the original question was, "find your passion in Life." You can then learn to appreciate the uniqueness of you. All the years of searching for answers had rendered him symbolically blind, and now he had been gifted with sight.

As you share Santosh's life, your senses are aroused by beautiful descriptions — "Despite being so late at night, the city didn't rest, it was never quiet." I learned about cast systems in India, as previously, I have only a spattering of understanding.

And yes, Santosh, "unconditional love does exist."

Congratulations on a thoughtful, helpful, quiet book. I hope many readers get to share your journey with you.

Judith Flitcroft. Author. Melbourne.

*   *   *

A personal journey of self-discovery, sharing profound wisdom and love along the way. Insightful reflections on achieving inner peace.

Review Vivian Waring (author *When Tears Ran Dry*)

*   *   *

I was completely engrossed from the first page. The extraordinary story telling transported me into Author's life starting as a small boy in Kerala with so many questions to this successful corporate executive in Biotechnology in Melbourne.

Then the dramatic shift occurs, with the narration of the health scare, which creates a very different mood and the story moves into a deeper self reflection phase.

The author then beautifully shares his transformation journey, where the search for meaning takes him into exploring a deeper dimension of life. Finally to top it all the author gently and deftly handles the most difficult question of all — the difficult question of who we truly are in very subtle, easy to understand words and analogies which one can easily relate .

I found the book easy to read, yet profound in its simplicity. The storytelling was very authentic and some of the characters in the book seemed so relatable. I really got a lot from it.

Sandeep Chitale.

Senior VP at VIS GLOBAL Pty Ltd. Australia.

Qualified Mindfulness practitioner through SIYLI/Googles Engage Program

*   *   *

Through the book — *The Art of Conscious Balance* , which is based on real life experience, Author, Santosh Nambiar has tried to explore his deepest feelings and emotions in a simple yet fearless manner. This is a beautiful account of the transformational change resulting in a whole new life of meaning and self awareness. There are several key pointers to those interested to adopt, learn and practice for their own journey to inner peace. Today, when people are trying to "change the world" we live in, the author's idea of changing our inner self is a powerful message for everlasting happiness.

Jithesh Janrdhanan.

Product Development TechnologistProduct Development Technologist

Fonterra, Australia

*   *   *

My first attempt at a cursory glance through *The Art of Conscious Balance* failed miserably. Every page I turned to, beckoned me to read it fully. Pretty soon I realised that I could not afford to miss any of the numerous gems scattered throughout this marvellous personal account of a man possessed, who chooses to lose, and wins. So I began from the beginning. From the simple parable of the crow who refuses to let go, I followed Santosh's journey, slowly unpeeling the layers of my being. Gradually, I found myself travelling with Santosh, with ever deeper self-awareness. As I meandered in the gently weaving flow of conscious balance, I found my own journey within. This book cannot be read. It must be experienced.

Vinay Nigam — Director — Academy of Professional Excellence

Melbourne Australia.

Emotional Intelligence certified Practitioner.

*   *   *

Are the choices that you make in life educated decisions or random ones? An intensely personal account, Santosh effortlessly essays his decisions and experiences in life in his latest book *The Art of Conscious Balance*. There are many times when one is at crossroads and the path chosen is purely "conscious" intuition. This essence comes out in this tough to put down book. Great reading!

Prof Sudha Warrier.

Professor and Dean at School of Regenerative Medicine Bangalore India.

*   *   *

The Art of Conscious Balance

BREAKING FREE FROM YOUR CONDITIONED SELF

The Art of Conscious Balance

BREAKING FREE FROM YOUR CONDITIONED SELF

SANTOSH NAMBIAR

Published in Australia by Sid Harta Books & Print Pty Ltd,
ABN: 34632585293
23 Stirling Crescent, Glen Waverley, Victoria 3150 Australia
Telephone: +61 3 9560 9920
E-mail: author@sidharta.com.au

First published in Australia 2021
This edition published 2021
Copyright © Santosh Nambiar 2021
Cover design, typesetting: WorkingType (www.workingtype.com.au)

Nambiar, Santosh
The Art of Conscious Balance
ISBN: 978-1-925707-72-4
pp242

Acknowledgments

First, I would like to thank my daughter, Sanjana Nambiar, who, with her intense research, creative and narrative writing style, helped shape this book. Our many dialogues during our evening stroll in the Wilson Botanic Park, Berwick, in Melbourne, has contributed immensely in shaping this book. Thank you, Molu.

I wish to thank the many friends, relatives, and acquaintances who came into my life. Each and every person has helped me become aware of the deep-rooted conditioned 'self' that kept me imprisoned. These individuals assisted me on my journey of self-discovery. Some of them include Radha Madhavan (Mads, Singapore), Amit Mathur, Ravi Ram Mohan, Ananth, Dr. B.P. Sreenivas, Dr. S. Ghosh and K.C.K Menon in India, Tom Verghese, Khamseng Sengsouvanh, Sue Block, Kiah, Jay, and Sandeep Chitale in Melbourne, the Pillais from Dunedin, Swamy and family in Auckland, Amanda Cameron in Auckland, Joe Keller in Mesquite, USA, and John Johnstone in Perth. As well as many, many other incredible individuals whose names I have not been able to include here.

My loving wife, Sandhya, who nursed me back to life from my illness, inspired me to embrace life despite the challenges and showed me the meaning of true unconditional love.

My brother Harish (Chicago, USA) and sister Indu (Sacramento, USA) for their tremendous support, love and affection during this complicated and confronting journey of self-discovery.

My dearest children, Sanjana and Sanjit, who always came to my support whenever I needed it most. I've learned quite a bit from their innocence, and they continue to inspire me.

My in-laws for their unrelenting support and unconditional love.

Jessica Bryan from Oregon, who looked through my initial drafts, and with skilful expertise selected the stories that were worth giving life. Thank you, Jessica, for your invaluable contributions towards this book and for your immense patience.

Sandy Draper for listening to my story with patience and accommodating all my requests while editing this book and making it a meaningful read. The collaboration was indeed one in which there was a lot of learning. Thank you, Sandy, for the excellent work despite the pandemic lockdown challenges in the UK.

Rebecca Wylie from Melbourne, for her valuable guidance on shaping the vital elements of this book. Thank you, Rebecca.

I am very grateful to Regina Lane and Liz Harrington for the final proofread. Thank you Regina and Liz.

I would like to especially thank Luke Harris from WorkingType Studio for all his support throughout the publishing process. I am very grateful for his valuable guidance, suggestions, patience and understanding throughout the journey. Thank you Luke.

Kerry B. Collison, Barbara Ivusic and Susan Keyssecker— at the Sid Harta Publishing House (Melbourne) for their kind support with the publishing of this book.

Lastly, my loving parents for giving us children space, patience, and freedom to explore and grow into the people we are today. Without their guidance and support, nothing would have been possible.

Finally, ever grateful to the eternal knowing, which I call 'the Universal Intelligence'. I realise that I am a mere tiny conduit for its immense power.

Foreword

We all stumble over the truth from time to time but most of us ignore it and carry on as if nothing happened. Santosh is an uncommon man who didn't ignore those moments of awakening and has used them as a compass to navigate his way through life and towards self-knowledge. In this book he has lovingly shared some of his insights and lessons that may inspire many others to find their inner compass to understand oneself and one's place in the universe more deeply and truly.

Professor Craig Hassed MBBS, FRACGP, OAM
Faculty of Medicine, Nursing and Health Sciences
Medical Education
Coordinator of Mindfulness at Monash
Faculty of Arts: Monash Centre for Consciousness and Contemplative Studies
Director of Education
Monash University
Australia

With lots of love and affection
to my Achan and Amma.

Contents

Preface

Sometime in my childhood, I heard a story about a crow and a wise owl, which stuck in my memory. The story goes as follows ...

One day, a crow managed to find a piece of meat. It held it in its beak with all its might. Up above, the eagles noticed the crow carrying the meat, and started to chase the crow. Desperately trying to escape the mighty eagles, the crow landed on a tree. A wise owl in the tree noticed the crow's anxiety and fear and asked what had happened. The crow explained to the owl that it was being chased by eagles. The owl said to the crow, 'The eagles are not chasing you. They are after the meat you are carrying in your beak. Drop that meat, and the eagles will not chase you anymore.' So, the crow dropped the meat and escaped to freedom.

The story did not make much sense to me as a child, but I now see its significance. Like many, I began my journey in life with the desire to achieve and accumulate. I aspired to success: a prestigious job, power, money, a top-of-the-line car, and a house in an affluent neighbourhood. There's nothing wrong with having ambitious dreams. However, I was trying to find joy and a sense of attainment with these goals. Possessing material wealth and fame spurred my sense of self. In fact, it did enhance my sense of self. But it was transient, and I felt incomplete despite achieving many of my dreams. There was always something missing in my life.

Unbeknownst to me, while earning this material wealth, I also accumulated anger, fear, an overbearing ego, arrogance, jealousy, and didn't care for other people's sensitivities. If I achieved what I set out to do—which often involved confronting or competing with others—I was happy.

In early 2002, everything changed. I was diagnosed with a serious illness and went through a period of intense suffering. For the first time, I was reminded of my mortality and the transient nature of all beings, including my own physical form. This profound experience triggered a shift within me, resulting in a deeper self-awareness and appreciation of life. My priorities realigned. I was finally attuned to life. I no longer had the urge to acquire material possessions, rejoice in my achievements, enhance my sense of self or convince others of my abilities.

For the first time, I asked myself some fundamental questions: Why do most of us struggle so much? Why do we feel incomplete, even amid worldly comfort? Why are we full of sorrow and frustration with our mediocre lives? As children, we were bundles of joy, so why do we become so filled with confusion, negativity, and disappointment in adulthood?

I realised that I had been selfish throughout my life. I am still selfish. But I am now more aware of my selfishness. This awareness makes me less selfish than I was before, aware that it is not all about me, and that I should consider others' wellbeing as well. This is a work in progress for me.

The mind, which I call 'intellect', is essential for our survival. Without it, we would become dysfunctional. But if we want to flourish and blossom, we need the guidance of something more than intellect. We need Universal Intelligence. Understanding how to pave a path between the intellect and Universal Intelligence is what I call the art of 'The art of Conscious Balance'. Practising it can help us become better human beings. The change within helps to change the world outside.

I now understand that real joy comes from being our true inner selves. Of course, material things matter to an extent, but being your true self is the only absolute. When this truth dawned on me, when I lost my attachment to material goods and worldly pleasures, the joy came from within.

I have finally realised the significance of the story of the crow and the wise owl. We are born as beautiful, joyous, pure beings. As we grow up, we tend to put on a facade—everything is about ourselves. A facade with all the conditioned baggage we have acquired during our upbringing—sorrows, hurts, angers, insecurities, anxieties, fears, and so on. This facade overpowers the joyous and pure being we once were and dominates our lives. During my period of introspection, I recognised this facade and saw my true, uncorrupted inner being shining through.

The piece of meat in the story is the baggage we have become conditioned to carry that conceals the true, pure grace within each of us. The burdensome weight of our past cause anxiety, stress, and fear. Once we realise this truth, once we stop identifying with this baggage (our facade), or at least become aware of its falseness, we can free ourselves from its clutches.

Absolute freedom is freedom from the conditioned mind. This is a simple truth. But it's not as easy as the crow dropping the morsel of meat. We are creatures of habit. It took a lot of effort to become aware of my baggage. Perhaps because it had been ingrained at a young age. The process of becoming self-aware wasn't easy and challenged my conditioned behaviours and thoughts. It required constant attention from moment to moment, and became an ongoing process of maintaining awareness, allowing my true self to shine. But after a while, I got the hang of it, and it became second nature.

The mind is humankind's most incredible tool, but it can also consume us, keeping us trapped in memories of the past or imagining the future. These states cause us suffering, anxiety, and stress, and we become like wound-up springs. When the mind is in control, it can take us to a memory or a future moment in a fraction of a second.

'Can we gain control of the mind?' I asked myself. With a bit of practice, we can. If we gain control, we can choose to go back to the past or future when we need to. For example, if we need to plan a journey we must think about the future, but not beyond what is required. This awareness allows us to use the mind to our advantage, avoiding unnecessary stress and suffering. If used consciously, the mind is at our beck and call. If we are unconscious, the mind takes charge. But we have a choice. I chose the former, and now my life is better and more grounded.

Absolute freedom is the liberation from the conditioned mind, and consciousness is the innate state of humankind from birth. So why do we struggle with it when nature is at ease with it? The natural world is in order, and it is for us to harmonise with it. Why doesn't this come naturally? I have heard people say that to do this, we must live in the present moment. We can, after all, only live in the present moment. Occasionally, we can also bring our mind to the present. During these times we experience joy but find it difficult to sustain this way of living. To do so, we need to become more aware of the mind's movement, which comes with practice.

The more I ask myself, 'How conscious am I in this moment?', I bring in a deeper awareness of my own conditioned behaviours. When I am sitting alone and become aware that my mind has strayed to a past or future event, I become conscious of my thinking—the noise in the mind—and then it quiets. In that silence, there is clarity. I am totally in the present. I am alert, attentive, and aware. There is clarity to what I hear, see, and feel, and a heightened sense of perception, which I call '360-degree awareness'. I begin to listen for the smallest noises—the ticking of a clock, the humming of the refrigerator, the wood creaking in the wind, the birds singing in the distance, a car engine fading away, the murmur of my own breathing. At these times, I become present. I see the true beauty of a flower and feel the breeze on my face.

These moments can be felt simultaneously in that silence. The moment we become oblivious to the present, the ticking becomes increasingly faint. Then I know I have moved away from the present moment and back into thinking about the past or future. This is my benchmark of moving away from the present moment.

I wish I undertook this self-discovery a long time ago. I wish I realised this simple truth when I was a child. Why didn't anyone tell me? Why don't schools talk about this? Instead of experiencing intense physical and mental suffering, wouldn't it be better to realise the joy of the present moment much earlier in life?

My self-inquiry, the inwardly focused journey, was challenging. It took considerable attentiveness to realise the extent of my own ignorance. Throughout life, many people assisted me with this life-changing experience. Each individual helped me delve deeper within myself, encouraging me to ask more probing questions to shed light on the layers of my mind-conceived ignorance. I am grateful to everyone who patiently supported me, helping me to change my life forever. The experience has been profound and remains a work in progress.

The following chapters share my own personal experience, and my hope is that it will help you to take your own inner journey. My intention is not to tell you what to do or how to do it. This journey of self-discovery is something each of us must experience through introspection. My journey and experience are entirely mine, and your journey may be completely different. As it is said, there are several paths to the truth, but the absolute truth will always be the same. I hope my experience may inspire, or at least plant, a seed of self-realisation within you.

Any words used to express the truth will fall short because language is manifested by the mind and therefore dwells in duality. It is like tasting honey for the first time and trying to explain that unique experience to another person in words. The words do not do justice to the experience, and the other person is unable to comprehend the significance of the memory. The truth defies description. But I hope these stories may guide you towards the absolute truth, inspiring self-realisation.

Thus, like the crow in the story, we need to be constantly aware of mind-conceived conditioned behaviours that keep us trapped. Think of it like shining a light on the dark corners of the mind and clearing away any cobwebs. All my life, I always believed that I was right and that the world around me needed correction. I have realised that the correction must happen within us. The cleansing needs to occur within. Then the world outside us also changes for the better. With that awareness comes what I call 'the six C's':

Consciousness, Clarity, Creativity, Calmness, Compassion & Connectedness

Most importantly, we become conscious, inspiring a more joyous, thriving and purposeful life. A mindful living.

Becoming mindful doesn't mean that life becomes free of stress, anxiety, anger and frustration. But it can help cope with life's chaotic situations, like the difficulties created by the COVID-19 pandemic. The struggle continues, but our responses to it can be significantly changed for the better.

While all this may sound a bit verbose, all I need to do is be in a state of presence, with conscious awareness, and the rest falls into place by the grace of the divine Intelligence.

Santosh Nambiar

Melbourne, Australia, 2021

One

Shadows in the Dark

*The rich suffer like the poor. There might be different reasons,
but they suffer just the same. Everyone suffers from anxiety,
jealousy, anger, fear and other negative emotions.*

I was born in Kannur, a tiny village in Kerala, in the southernmost state of India. Thinking of my hometown brings back vivid images of vast, verdant paddy fields lined with tall, regal coconut trees. Warm tropical winds drifted through the quaint village—and in the fields, an abundance of vibrant, yellow bananas hung ripe for the picking.

We children would run through the tall grasses of the paddy fields and splash through puddles, kicking an old soccer ball. The whole village was our playground. No tree remained unclimbed and our bare feet were comfortingly familiar with the soft, fertile soil carpeting the fields. From rising at the break of dawn until the moment we returned home at dusk, we raced through the fields playing countless games.

We plucked mangoes from the trees' broad branches—the

succulent golden fruits were our primary source of food during the day. There was no stress and nothing to worry about. We simply embraced the moment, living at ease in a world of our own. Our longing for adventure and a sense of camaraderie propelled us. We considered ourselves equals—to each other and to the natural world that surrounded us.

*   *   *

Late one day, as the sun was beginning to set, I made my way home through the paddy fields, being careful to avoid the snakes waiting to catch frogs. Several lazy cows looked up, following me wide-eyed, before resuming grazing. A few, having eaten their fill, were lying on the soft carpet of lush, green grass that had grown taller after the monsoon rains. Among them, tiny black-and-white spotted calves chased the crows drinking dew from the long blades of grass.

Passing the large mango tree where I often played with my friends, I noticed some squirrels nibbling on the fresh fruit that had fallen on the ground the night before. As I continued walking, the intense smell of roasting coconut and chillies from a nearby home delighted my senses. Someone was cooking dinner! Otherwise, the evening serenity was only broken by the occasional sound of a woodpecker searching for food and the cry of a crow pheasant flying overhead.

*   *   *

When I arrived home, ravenous and exhausted, my grandmother reprimanded me for playing with the children who lived on the other side of the village. My grandmother was a traditional old woman. A woman who had been forced to obey our cultural norms and customs early in life. It had been her responsibility to raise her children to heed these norms, and now she would do the same for her grandchildren. 'Santosh, how many times have I told you?' she said. 'You are not to play with those children.' My grandfather sat at the head of the table, patiently ignoring my grandmother's anger, enjoying his meal after a laborious day taking care of the family estate and lands.

I listened, confused by her insistence. But as I was about to respond, my mother's stony glare shut me up. I looked towards my grandfather, who looked at me curiously, his eyes willing me to be patient with my grandmother. I didn't understand why I wasn't allowed to play with some of my friends. They were equally fun and shared the same excitement and curiosity for the world as the other children. Especially Raju—he was the best. Raju had shown me the mango tree in the isolated grove behind his house, where the most succulent specimens hid. Every spring, the two of us went to the grove and climbed the sweeping branches to pick the ripe, swaying fruit, and then eat our fill. I honestly didn't understand my grandmother and didn't heed her advice. I continued to play with all my friends. But somehow, my grandmother always found out, and I wondered whether she was spying on me. Some days when I was playing in the fields with my friends,

I looked around to see if her stooped, fluffy white-haired figure was watching.

One afternoon as I sat on the earth beside a field of coconut trees, waiting for my grandfather as he talked with the labourers who worked for him, I noticed something different about him. As a landowner, my grandfather inherited ample land from his ancestors, despite the rise of Communism in Kerala a few years ago. What struck me as interesting was how he interacted with his workers. I watched as he stood amongst them, talking and laughing, as his equals. My grandmother considered the poor labourers and their children inferior to us, yet I failed to notice the countless times my grandfather treated them with respect. The times he would give them extra money for their work, the generous abundance of agricultural supplies that he provided them, the food, clothes, and support that he generously offered. Those innocent moments where he would eat his lunch with them as an equal, despite the entrenched social beliefs about caste. It was these subtle acts of kindness that earned my grandfather respect from his men and workers, eventually leading to his role as their esteemed father figure.

As the sunlight waned, my grandfather called for me and we walked back home. I followed his large, confident strides. 'Grandfather, why are you friends with your workers?' I asked innocently. He turned to look at me as we walked, never missing a step. He stayed silent, allowing me to continue. 'Grandma doesn't let me play with their children, yet you treat these men like family. Why?'

He turned around and smiled, 'They are people just like us, that's why,' and he continued walking as I followed him with a newfound respect for my wise grandfather.

Unfortunately, less than a year later, my kind-hearted grandfather passed on when his body failed him, leaving me to believe and defend his views on humanity. The day after my grandfather passed, I felt lost. He had been a constant source of guidance and reassurance. I missed his kind, smiling face over the dinner table and the calming timbre of his voice. Unable to sit in the silent and grieving house, I left early in the morning. I walked past our flourishing fields of vegetation. Fields that my grandfather tended to for years. Land that he loved and nurtured. My heart weighed heavily in my chest as I walked past the empty fields. I kept walking for what felt like hours. I needed some space. I decided to take a less trodden path—an unknown path. I wanted to find a place where I could breathe and come to peace with my grief.

The sun beat down on the earth. Shading my eyes, I looked up towards the horizon. That's when I noticed it—the broken hill. A halo of light surrounded the lonely crest of the hill. Up against the backdrop of the infinite blue sky, the outline of the hill seemed almost geometric. Perfect angles that cut into the sky. Almost like the hill had been broken, cracked off from the land. From where I stood, it was magnificent. Tall and majestic above the valley and fields below. It was like an undiscovered land, a place where nothing could get to me, a place of escape.

It was high up from the ground and a steep climb up. On my

hands and knees, I trekked to the top. I gripped onto the crevices between rocks and pulled out plants to help me up—dirt covered my palms and knees and they were scratched from the endeavour. Eventually, I stumbled to the top, hands on my legs, hunched forward, heaving from the effort. I looked up and realised the climb had been worth it.

The sun bid farewell in pink and orange hues that floated in the sky and fell upon the tiny village beneath. The warm, golden light lit up the fields and reflected against the still waters of the saturated paddy fields. A cargo train rumbled in the distance, and I sat on top of my hill, watching everything. It was beautiful. I moved forwards to the edge, trying to see if I could see my house from the hill. But something in my peripheral vision caught my attention.

A single yellow flower. It budded from a little bush at the crest of the hill. The flower stood tall and proud at the hill's very tip, its petals wide and porcelain-smooth, straining towards the last light.

I stayed on the hill, watching the activity below. It was a perfect place of peace. As the sun disappeared, I realised it was time to go, so I treaded back down the hill, skidding on the soft soil and sliding down half the way. I smiled, proud of my newly discovered place, knowing that it would be my special place. A place that no one else knew. As I turned to look at it one last time, the yellow flower at the top of the broken hill dipped its head in farewell as the final ray of light disappeared for the day.

*   *   *

Despite my grandfather's death, my grandmother did not change. I grew tired of hearing her concerns about who I was friends with and the way I treated our workers. To my grandmother, the established rules on classism were set in stone and nothing would change her mind. I remembered my grandfather and his values about equality. 'What's wrong with those children?' I would say. 'They're people just like us with families. Just because their house doesn't look like ours, or their last name is different from ours, doesn't make them different. It makes no sense to avoid them.'

I tried to talk about it with my mother, hoping she would take my side. But she agreed with my grandmother. 'They're not from the same caste as us,' she said. Seeing my confused expression, she continued, 'There's a hierarchy in our society. Our family and our ancestors are higher. Those friends you play with are not your equals, so you should not associate with them. It's against the rules that govern our society.' I was about to say something about how backwards it all was, but my mother added, 'Just listen to your grandmother; she knows what she's talking about. You'll understand when you're older.'

It made no sense. Even as I grew into adolescence, I found the whole social institution regarding the caste system to be primitive and, honestly, messed up. I hoped my grandmother was wrong. I missed my grandfather more than ever during these times. But even when he was alive, he had never been able to change his wife. In fact, he always expressed his compassion quietly, helping people with no expectations in return and always forgiving others despite their opposing views. But I knew that my grandmother and the wider society were being callous and unfair, and I would stand up for my innocent friends despite what anyone said.

However, despite my incessant quest for justice, nothing changed—the rich grew richer and the poor poorer, while my grandmother's ingrained values about classism remained intact.

Two

The Seed of Hope

The question you must ask first — probably one of the hardest of all — is: Who am I? Who am I really?

 One weekend morning, I woke reluctantly, wishing I could join my friends for our usual morning swim at the swimming pond. However, my closest friend Madhavan, who lived next door, somehow persuaded me to join him and his father to listen to a spiritual guru in the town hall of a neighbouring village. I wasn't all that keen, but 'Mads' (as I fondly called him) was desperate for company.

Mads and his father took the bus, but I decided to cycle. It was a pleasant ride along empty narrow streets and the cool morning breeze was refreshing. When I reached the neighbouring village, Chala, Mads and his dad were getting off the bus. We were a bit early, so Mads' father took us to a little tea shop next to the bus stop. We sat down on the rickety wooden bench to drink our tea, the three of us precariously balancing on it.

When Mads' father looked at his watch, it was almost time for the guru's lecture, so we quickly finished our tea and hurried to the town hall. By the time we got there, the crowds were already filing in, so we followed. We sat down on the blanketed floor, a few rows from the front. Mads and I looked at each other with shared disdain as silence fell and the guru walked towards the stage. I learned that the guru was fondly called RG, or Arjee, by his followers, and was well known for his oration and ability to break complex concepts into simple pointers for life.

We listened patiently to his discourse on compassion and the difference between unconditional love and the conditional love that society embraces, and then a question-and-answer session began. Some of the audience were keen and raised their hands. The guru answered one tricky question after another, while one key question continued to flicker in my mind. I was eager to ask the guru, but for some reason, I couldn't find the courage to stand up in the crowd. I wasn't sure if it would be met with confusion or disapproval because I was a child. Even more, I wasn't sure if the question was apt. Just as I was contemplating whether I should or not, trying to work up the courage, my hand shot up, seemingly of its own accord, and I heard my voice ring out across the room: 'Why doesn't my grandma allow me to play with some of my friends? Is that because they are poor or socially from a low social status? Why is there so much suffering and discrimination within our society?'

I leaned forward intently. Mads looked at me, smirking, but I decided to ignore him. The guru smiled and stared at me, and then nodded his head —a knowing expression on his face. 'This question is fundamental and I'm glad someone so young has taken the time to contemplate something so complex, yet so vital. Suffering, you say? And you are right in using that word—suffering, it is indeed. You are also right in assuming that everyone in our society suffers. So, if everyone suffers, there must be something we are all doing wrong.' He looked at me for a moment, pausing to gather his thoughts before speaking again: 'Child, I cannot answer this question for you. You must discover the solution for yourself. However, what you must ask first—probably hardest of all—is: "Who am I? Who am I really?" Ponder over it. I want you to discover the answer for yourself. This answer can lead you to the reason why humanity suffers.'

I thought: *Who am I? What's so difficult about that? I am Santosh, twelve years old. How does this answer my question? I already know who I am.*

Feeling a bit disappointed, I remained quiet, but his words continued to run through my mind.

Mads was thoroughly amused by my audacity and my interest in what the spiritual teacher had said. 'It took me so long to make you come with me,' Mads said. 'I had to bribe you by buying you an ice-cream. Now look who's the interested one. Are you going to be a guru when you grow up?'

I rolled my eyes and punched him playfully on the shoulder.

Three

Love in Action

Unconditional love has no expectations.
It is pure and untainted by the mind.

Mads and his dad went home on the afternoon bus, and I pedalled home at a leisurely pace. The brutal sun beat down and sweat ran down my flushed face. Longing for a cool glass of water, I stopped and parked my bike next to a wooden gate. On the other side of it there was a modest, cream-coloured home surrounded by a manicured lawn. The long limbs of a large tree with dense leaves grew in the corner. Arching towards the house, it provided cool shade.

I tugged on a little bell hanging from the pillar by the gate, and it emitted a loud ping. Waiting patiently, I looked at the house, hoping someone was inside. Then the door opened, and a middle-aged man with greying hair and kind eyes walked out onto the verandah. He wore a faded blue shirt and a clean, white dhoti. He peered at me curiously and, seeing my bike, smiled, motioning for me to come inside. So I pushed the gate aside and stepped in.

'Hello, sir, I don't mean to intrude, but I was wondering whether you would give me some water?'

The man continued smiling. 'Of course. You must be tired and thirsty. It is so hot today, and it's not good to be out in the sun too long. My name is Abdul. Please come inside.' He pointed to a chair on his front verandah, indicating I should sit, and then he called out, 'Amit, can you please get our guest some water?'

A boy, about my age, came out with two glasses. 'My son, Amit,' said the man with evident pride.

I took the water from Amit's outstretched hand. After gulping it down, I stared at the empty glass.

Abdul smiled and seemed amused, as if he knew what I was thinking. 'Here,' he said, 'take my glass. I'll ask Amit for more.' I drank the water gratefully, satiating my extreme thirst.

'Where are you going?' Abdul asked as he looked at my bike. I explained that I had visited a nearby village to listen to a spiritual guru. I told him about how I had asked the guru a question and how the guru hadn't given me a proper answer.

'What did you ask the guru?' he said.

'I don't understand why I can play with some children and not with others in my village. Why is there such division within society? Why are my friends' unequal? Why are there castes? Why are some of my friends rich while others are poor and suffering, and why does no one seem to care?'

'Did you receive a satisfactory answer?'

'The guru answered my question with another question! He told me to ask myself, "Who am I?", and said by answering this question, my other questions might also be answered.'

Abdul listened intently. No one had ever listened to me so graciously and allowed me to express my views, except for my grandfather. This was one of the downfalls of being young— although we had no worries, adults usually behaved as though we were also undeserving of respect.

As our conversation deepened, I learned that Abdul was a farmer, like his ancestors before him. He had a thriving field of crops but, sadly, was a widower. His beautiful, kind wife had died over ten years before. But he wasn't alone. He had three children—a boy and two young girls.

As the sun's rays faded, Abdul went to prepare dinner. Getting up, I told him I needed to go home.

'Santosh, please stay and eat dinner. You must be hungry, and it is too late to ride home. You can stay with us and continue on in the morning.'

Although I was keen to get home, I couldn't resist the warm charm radiating from Abdul and his home. He let me use his telephone to call my mother, who was worried about me riding at night. And so, it was decided.

I joined Abdul and his children for dinner on the floor of one of his house's two rooms, one being the tiny kitchen and the other a square living area that led out to the open verandah at the front of the house. Abdul served a simple meal: thick rice porridge, yellow dahl with spinach, and a rich spicy curry made with coconut milk. I ate well and thoroughly enjoyed the food. When I yawned, Abdul ushered me to a bed near the open verandah and offered a blanket to protect me from the cool, night breeze.

*   *   *

I woke to pale light streaming into the room. I sat up, dazed, stretching my arms over my head as my brain recollected yesterday's events. My throat was parched, so I went to get a drink. Padding across the cool, bare floor towards the kitchen, I noticed a large bed in the open living area that hadn't been there the night before. Abdul's three children were sleeping soundly, comforted by a thick blanket. When I looked to the side, I noticed Abdul sleeping peacefully on a jute mat on the floor. A thin blanket barely covered his large body.

After drinking some water, I checked my little watch. It was a quarter-past five. Before leaving, I wrote a message to Abdul and his children, thanking them for their warm hospitality and delicious food. I didn't want to wake them, so I left the note on the verandah beneath a rock and pedalled home, enjoying the early morning ride. The sun hadn't fully risen; a crust of bright orange was beginning to spill its rays across the landscape and the early birds announced the arrival of the new day.

On my way home, I thought about the guru's question: 'Who am I?' It made no more sense than it had the day before. But then I heard his voice resonating in my mind. Something he had said in his discourse: 'Unconditional love has no expectations. It is pure and untainted by the mind.'

I thought about Abdul and how caring and compassionate he had been to me, a tired young boy. I was deeply moved by how he'd looked after me as if I was one of his own children and how he expected nothing in return.

Unconditional love really does exist, after all, I thought.

Four

Perfect Made Imperfect

Donning the mask.

My world changed when my parents moved to a larger town called Karaikudi in another state of India named Tamil Nadu. I was around twelve years old and yearning for adventure, so the prospect was exciting. I had never been far from Kannur, and the world felt large and endless. I was especially looking forward to the journey because we would travel by train.

Trains fascinated me. I would watch them as they slowly travelled over the tracks and then disappeared into the distance. I wondered about the people on the train. Where were they going and why? As each train vanished behind the rolling hills, I longed to be on it and going somewhere.

Finally, the day came. We packed our bags and loaded our furniture onto a truck. I ran through the only home I had ever known, saying a silent goodbye. With a heavy heart, I said goodbye to my friends, knowing I would miss playing and exploring with them. I playfully punched Mads' shoulder, trying to hold the emotion back. Raju handed me a perfect, golden mango as a goodbye gift, reminiscent of the summer when we found the lucky mango tree. Despite my sadness at leaving, I was filled with excitement and curiosity for the new life ahead. As the train moved out of the station, I watched my village fly past until it was entirely gone from view.

*   *   *

Settling into the new town wasn't as easy as I anticipated, and I struggled to adapt to our new home and surroundings. I had no friends and didn't know the language. At my previous school, we spoke in the native language of the state of Kerala: Malayalam. At my new school, they spoke English, which I had never encountered before, and it was nearly impossible to communicate with my new teachers and schoolmates. Feeling alone, I would think back to my old friends and long to be splashing around in the massive emerald pool behind our houses or playing tag in the endless fields.

My teachers showed little sympathy for the challenges I faced. They merely expected me to keep up. Unable to express myself and lacking support, my confidence waned. I became reclusive and inhibited. I was also angry—with everyone and at myself. When the teachers asked me questions, I sat in numb silence, unable to comprehend, while the other students giggled, seeming to revel in my embarrassment. I felt humiliated and belittled, and the teachers showed no compassion. I could only sit in my seat, straining to make sense of the stream of words coming from their mouths. Nothing made any sense, and I could never finish my homework because of my inability to understand what was expected.

Fearing the teachers' ridicule as they looked at my book's blank pages, I often skipped class, hiding on the roof at home. A tree leaned towards the house with strong, sturdy branches, creating a perfect path to the top of the house. Suffice to say, my years of tree climbing were put to use. I would sit, watching as people passed by, completely oblivious to my presence. I eventually came back down when the afternoon sun settled low on the landscape.

My parents always stressed the importance of education, and now I was failing right in front of them. Over time, my poor performance became a habit. The teachers seemed to give up on me, which seemed unfair, considering they never tried to help me in the first place. Every class was a nightmare. Be it Mathematics, English, or Science, I got consistently low marks on all tests and end-of-year exams. Soon the teachers and my classmates labelled me as 'good for nothing'. Gradually this label stuck, ingrained in my mind. I believed I wasn't good enough.

*   *   *

In English class one day, I sat at my usual place in the corner, well out of the teacher's reach, trying to make sense of the lesson. Reading from a textbook and quoting some English scholar, the words tumbled out of her mouth and flew over my head. As a soft, warm breeze drifted through the open door, I daydreamed of my childhood in Kannur. I'm not sure what triggered the memory. Maybe it was a longing to feel free and happy again.

I missed the joy of playing from early morning until the last amber rays of the sun disappeared. We played hide-and-seek, tag, soccer, marbles and made-up games with stones and branches; we even climbed trees. We had endless space to play—acres and acres of paddy fields with graceful coconut trees standing proud across the skyline. We were carefree, with all the time in the world. We had no leader, no parents to supervise us, and yet everything fell perfectly into place. We agreed with each other about the day's game and which tree to climb. And when we were tired, one of the leafy mango trees provided a perfect canopy and respite from the hot sun.

Now, trapped in the city in a stifling classroom, I thought about how we would wait eagerly for a strong wind to bring down five or more mangoes. Each of us would race to get one, although often the fruit would already have been partly eaten by the squirrels. Disappointed and hungry, we would wait for another forceful wind to shake the tree.

Suddenly the teacher called my name, jerking me back to the present. I shook my head to clear my mind, momentarily confused as the green landscape of Kannur faded, revealing the dull classroom with its wooden benches. Everyone was staring at me with a combination of amusement and pity. The teacher walked down the aisle towards me. I looked down, avoiding eye contact. She asked me to stand at the front of the class and read a poem from the book. I don't think she meant to punish me but rather to challenge me.

My heart hammered and my breathing became fast and shallow as I stood. My stomach churned and my legs trembled as I stumbled slowly towards the front. I turned to face the class, aware of the teacher standing to the side watching. She nodded her head, prompting me to read. Staring down at the words, sweat beaded my forehead and suddenly my entire face flushed. Several pairs of eyes stared straight at me.

I opened my mouth to read the first word. Nothing. The words stuck in my throat, seeming to choke me. I tried it again. Nothing. Dejected and humiliated, I looked at the teacher in desperation. She turned away in disappointment and told me to sit down. Some of my classmates stifled giggles and pointed; others avoided my eyes, feeling pity and embarrassment. The teacher called up another student, who confidently walked past me and read the poem in perfect diction. I returned to my seat, hunched over, attempting to hide from my own humiliation. Holding back tears, I stared at the worn wooden desk, desperate to avoid any further attention.

This incident haunted me for years. I could not speak about, mostly because of the communication barrier, though no one was listening anyway. Although I was always surrounded by people, I felt that no one in the world could help me. I believed that no one was willing to listen to me or take the time to understand what I was going through. Negative emotions continued to bubble up, threatening to erupt, despite my efforts to suppress them.

*   *   *

Suffice to say, my time at school was challenging. I struggled and memorised redundant information to pass exams, but learning became a tedious task that I detested. I couldn't grasp the significance of what I was learning; it was just mounds of information with no meaning or relevance in my life.

Teachers stressed the importance of grades, praising those who got top marks while deriding those who performed poorly. However, I was proud of one accomplishment: learning English, a skill that would prove beneficial throughout my life. I could, after almost five years, finally understand my teachers and friends and express myself. When I eventually reached year eleven, I moved school again as mine didn't offer senior year levels. When I realised this, it sparked my sense of childhood adventure. The daily routine and familiarity of my present life were stifling, and I was beginning to dislike its mediocrity. I longed for change. New school, new friends, new teachers—all provided me with a fresh start.

Five

Under the Glow
of a Streetlight

Finding freedom, we set out to prove that we are worthy.

The new environment at senior school provided the impetus to do well. Moving schools became a blessing as I became motivated to excel academically. I wanted to succeed and prove to everyone that I was not 'good for nothing'. My marks improved, and this spurred my confidence. I worked hard on my subjects both at home and at school.

With ambition raging within me, sleeping ceased to be a priority, and sometimes I studied all night. Our neighbourhood's electricity failed frequently due to load-shedding, a term I knew because I grew up with constant power outages. Luckily the colony we grew up in had backup generators to light up the streetlights. I would study under the dim streetlight near my home—the golden light creating a yellow halo on the concrete pavement. I enjoyed the cool and quiet darkness while everyone else slept soundly, and the moon watched over the Earth with almost maternal, protective love.

Late into the night, the streetlight would sometimes begin to flicker, as if telling me it's time to go to sleep. I would just move over to the next streetlight and continue. I had this newfound determination, dedication, and discipline. I was relentless in my pursuit. When I look back at it now, I realise I just wanted to prove to the world that I was worthy.

My scores improved, and my teachers seemed to like me. I excelled in mathematics, physics, biology and physical education.

At times, the feeling of being 'good for nothing' would spring up, and for a moment, I would become the reclusive, isolated boy I once was. But as I grew courageous and slowly overcame the negative effects of my most profound insecurities, I was no longer that boy. I had taken control of my life. Or so I thought.

*   *   *

When I finished year twelve, I had no idea what to do next. School was easy. You did what you had to do; what people told you to do. Figuring out what happened next was hard. The questions tormented me. 'What are you doing next?' or 'What do you want to do in the future?' When asked, I would visibly bristle with annoyance: 'I don't know!' How was a seventeen-year-old boy meant to know what he wanted to do for the rest of his life? How could I envision my future when I was so confused about today? It was interesting that my years of schooling hadn't equipped me with a vision for my future.

When the time to choose inevitably came, my parents chose for me—Bachelor of Science. I was okay with that; I liked science and had attained a place at the university in Tamil Nadu.

University was fun. I made new friends, studied hard, my professors liked me, and I made a place for myself within the community. I felt I had finally proven my worth, and others respected and liked what they saw. I worked diligently, but when I completed the three-year course, I was again at a crossroad: *What do I do now?* So, I decided to keep going, keep studying. I enrolled in a master's degree in biology at the prestigious School of Biological Sciences, Madurai Kamaraj University (MKU) in Madurai, Tamil Nadu. My parents were supportive and proud. I guess they were happy to finally see me doing something; achieving.

I travelled to Madurai via three crowded buses. The five-hour journey was exhausting, and the stifling heat exacerbated the tediousness. Madurai was hot and dry, much like the rest of the state. Despite the arid climate it had an abundance of green life, reminding me of my village in Kerala. Massive mountains guarded the city, looming in the distance and sometimes overshadowed by clouds during the rainy season. Being an undergraduate had been exciting and freeing, but it didn't compare to my post-grad experience. I lived on campus in a dorm with two other students. Having shared a room all my life, this was fine by me. It was fun, living and studying with friends.

I was reunited with Mads, my childhood best friend. When we found out that we were both going to the same university, we were ecstatic. Mads hadn't changed—still as crazy, as full of life, and as adventurous as always. There was never a dull moment. Sometimes my father would visit, enduring the tedious journey across the state. Together we would walk for hours through the city before stopping at a street tea store to drink a cup of steaming sweet chai. Then as the sun began its descent, we would walk towards the bus stand. Each time before he boarded the bus, he gave me a quick pat on the back and put a wad of money in my hand. 'For anything you need,' he would say, as he stepped onto the bus. It was always a good day when he came.

We studied hard throughout the day, going to classes and lectures in the morning. The food at the dorm was excellent and abundant. Even so, we were always hungry. So, after dinner, a group of us would go out to the street food stores. Some days we would go to the nearest theatre to watch the latest Indian and Hollywood movie releases. It was these moments that we cherished and waited for.

After the movie finished late at night, we went for a long walk. Sometimes Mads persuaded me to go towards the mountain behind our university campus. It was risky; the mountain was known by locals as 'Snake Mountain'. But if snakes lurked within the long grasses, we never saw them and didn't fear them. We would walk higher and higher up the mountain, stumbling in the dark and laughing when one of us fell. When we finally reached a good height, we would sit on the dusty, rocky surface of the hill and look down at the bustling city beneath—the lights of the university campus, the soft murmur of voices as people walked across campus, the loud, demanding shouts of the street vendors, buses travelling with their loads of people to various destinations. Despite being so late in the night, the city didn't rest; it was never quiet.

*   *   *

My time at college passed quickly, and soon, everyone left on their own separate paths. Many went to pursue jobs in companies, hoping to earn some money and become financially independent. Others to continue their studies elsewhere. Still lost, but driven by a fire inside me, I continued to study, enrolling for PhD in Molecular Biology at the School of Biological Sciences, Madurai Kamaraj University. I wasn't ready to leave yet. But working for my PhD wasn't as enjoyable as I hoped. I missed my friends who'd left, and those remaining became more serious about their careers and studies. So, in the end, after enduring 3 years of PhD study, I dropped out of university, lured by the appeal of a lucrative career with a multinational biotech company based in Bangalore.

It was during my first job with a German multinational company based in Bangalore, that I had the opportunity of travelling overseas. I had travelled extensively within India. My first trip to Germany made me realise how vast the world truly is. I vividly recall watching through the window the vast and overcast Frankfurt city for the first time as the plane descended towards the magnificent city. After living in the heat and bustle of India, the silence and the clement weather was refreshing. I stayed in Frankfurt for the night. The next day I travelled to Penzberg. Penzberg is a small town in Bavaria, Germany, known for its coal mining and Pharmaceutical industries. As we drove from Frankfurt to Penzberg, I watched the scenery around me in awe. The landscapes of Germany are at once charming. Alpine peaks, mysterious forests, villages lined with timbered houses, and castles that seem almost too majestic to be real. Life in Germany seemed so peaceful, quiet and orderly. I knew then that I had to travel and explore more.

Six

Eyes on the Prize

Seeking happiness through material success,
do we ever stop to consider the price?

In 1996, I decided to emigrate to New Zealand. Once again, my childhood longing for adventure and discovery spurred me to travel and explore new places. I wanted to see the world, experience different cultures, and meet new people. My life in India was satisfying, but I wasn't challenged. I worked for one of the best multinational biotechnology companies, earning a handsome salary. I quickly moved up the corporate ladder, and my seniors were impressed by my insatiable ambition. Still, everything I did was about making sure I erased the label 'good for nothing'.

In the midst of my preparation of moving to New Zealand, I had begun thinking about marriage. The thought about marriage did not cross my mind previously. Since starting my first job, I had been to countless weddings. As I watched my friends settle into family life, I began to consider the possibility of inviting someone new into my life. Someone who would support my dream, who would grow with me, someone who yearned for adventure and was excited for life as I was. Though my parents and grandparents had been united through traditional arranged marriage, my generation had more freedom to choose our life partner. Though the process was an adaptation of the traditional arranged marriage, it gave individuals' the time and opportunity to get to know each other before they committed to marriage. When I met Sandhya, I immediately knew she was the one for me. She was quiet when I first met her but her eyes revealed the independent, strong-willed and deeply compassionate persona within. She was so full of life, curious and excited about everything. When I told her about my plan of moving to New Zealand, she seemed very excited. It didn't take long. I knew with utmost resolution that I had finally found my life-partner.

I was so proud the day I received permanent residency in New Zealand. The process wasn't easy. It took two years of preparation and filling out forms and meeting officials before the formalities and the paperwork were completed. As I prepared to leave, I rang up all my friends to let them know the big news. My parents were growing older and were unhappy with my decision, as it meant I would no longer be living nearby. I didn't try to understand their feelings. I set my mind on New Zealand, and I was going. Sadly, Sandhya had to stay back in India while I moved to New Zealand to find a job and to make a comfortable home for us.

Finally, the day came. My suitcase was packed with a few clothes and bare necessities. I wanted to start anew, so I left most of my belongings behind or gave them away. I looked around at my emptied apartment—the warm dusty air of Bangalore fanned the curtains and drifted through the house. I started my climb for corporate success in this city with my first real job, but now I was ready to soar across the world and become even more successful. With this determined thought in my head, I picked up my suitcase and walked out the door, locking it behind me.

*   *   *

The flight descended into Auckland. Grey clouds loomed above, in such contrast to India's scorching heat that I'd left behind. As I walked out of the airport, the unfamiliar environment, the quietness, the chilling winter breeze, and the uncertainty of my future, all seemed overwhelming.

I knew moving to New Zealand wouldn't be easy. After all, I left my job and arrived in New Zealand with little money, nowhere to live, and nothing certain regarding employment. Thankfully, a family took me in, but the facilities were not ideal. The tiny room was claustrophobic, and the grey walls seemed to cave in on the narrow bed. For the first few months, I took odd jobs to keep the money coming in. I was overqualified for most of the available positions, but I didn't care. I knew my time would come. I just had to keep working towards my dream.

*   *   *

41

Life in Auckland was vastly different from India—the lack of bustle and noise and the cold, dry climate and loneliness took their toll. My working life was also dramatically different.

My first position was in telephone sales. On the first day, I walked in with a positive mindset, but everything came crashing down after my first call was abruptly disconnected. By the end of the day, my initial determination had been replaced by rejection. I hadn't been able to get through to any of the customers, and most of them cut me off before I could say anything. Some of them even got angry and cursed at me. In the coming weeks, things didn't improve, and when the supervisor asked for my sales, I stared at the floor and told him my measly sum. Looking at me in dismay, he directed me to clean the kitchen or toilet as punishment. Slowly, the label 'good for nothing' resurfaced in my mind.

I continually looked for a better job, but was hindered by my mediocre English and lack of work experience. Finally, I found a job as a waiter working evenings in an Indian restaurant, and because the money wasn't enough to make ends meet, I got a second job during the day with a carpet cleaning company. Moving from house to house, carrying the heavy machines and then pushing them back and forth to clean and steam the carpets, was exhausting. By the end of the day, my back groaned in agony, and my body pleaded for rest. But then I had to rush home, take a quick shower, and put on my uniform for the restaurant. After the restaurant closed late at night, I cleaned and vacuumed and rushed back home to sleep for a couple of hours before another tedious day began.

On Tuesdays and Thursdays, my days off, I perused the local newspapers' employment pages, looking for work in the life sciences industry. Each week, I applied for around twenty positions, ranging from lab assistant to sales manager. Each application resulted in a standard typed response stating they evaluated my CV but found a more suitable candidate. Although initially disheartening, I saw my future in front of me. I just had to run to reach it.

After a few months in New Zealand, I felt at home. I got used to the freezing winter and chilling winds. I enjoyed the absolute freedom of being in a new city and immersed myself in the culture, the new way of life, and started making friends.

One day, after working a full night at the restaurant, I returned home to a pile of mail. Tired and reluctant to open any of it, I stumbled into bed. I woke up at around five in the morning to get ready for my carpet-cleaning job. As I walked out of the shower, I noticed the letters again. I picked up and opened each envelope, one by one, and skimmed through them—*Unfortunately. Another candidate. Sorry.*

When I picked up the final letter and skimmed the words, it took my brain a few moments to register what they said. I stood up in excitement and reread the letter. I was being called for an interview by a recruiter. Finally, there was some hope. Immediately, I went through the multiple notes I prepared for any potential job interview. As I cleaned carpets that day, all I could think about was the interview scenario and how I would present myself.

After work, I rushed home and studied interview techniques. I carefully planned what I would wear and ironed my best clothes. I practised my handshake and posture in front of the mirror. My accent was a bit worrisome because it wasn't very polished. However, there was nothing I could do except be myself and try to appear confident.

When the day of the interview arrived, everything fell into place perfectly. I caught the bus to the destination and arrived on time. I felt and looked professional. Walking into the building, my back was straight. I maintained an easy facial expression, smiling with confidence. As I waited in the reception area, my mind whirled with thoughts. I worried about stumbling through the interview and embarrassing myself. I didn't want to fail; I needed to prove to myself I could do it. I didn't want to be trapped as a waiter and carpet cleaner for the rest of my life.

'Santosh Nambiar,' someone called.

Flustered, I stood up. Regaining composure, I nodded and smiled at a tall woman in a blue pinstriped pantsuit with greying auburn hair. She looked pleasant but detached, as if she didn't want to give anything away. I shook her hand firmly—as I had practised.

When I walked out of the building after the interview, I smiled with satisfaction. I had articulated well and presented myself as confident and reliable. Although I wanted the job, I wouldn't mind if I didn't get it, because this experience proved to me that I could interview successfully.

A few days later, I received a call from the recruiter asking for a second interview. She told me the job had been offered to someone else, but she forwarded my CV to another manager in the same company, and the manager was interested in meeting me.

Within a couple of weeks, I was offered the job. I signed all the documents and got ready to move from Auckland to Dunedin, on the South Island. Moving again wasn't an issue, considering that I had already flown from India to New Zealand. The company offered me the position of Account Manager based in Dunedin, as well as a company car and a brick-like Motorola mobile phone. I was incredibly proud of my accomplishment. The company also flew me to Dunedin, where I would begin another chapter of my life. I was finally on my way to realising my ambitions. A successful life suddenly seemed within my grasp.

*   *   *

As I stepped off the plane in Dunedin, I was met with strong, chilling winds. I was used to the cool weather of Auckland, but South Island was colder. Winter approached, and I wasn't adequately clothed for its arrival. I pulled my jacket tightly around me and hailed a cab.

For the first few weeks, I stayed at a motel in the city centre, which allowed me to explore the city. I bundled up with layers of jackets to face the biting wind. Dunedin is a small, picturesque city at the Otago Harbour head, with gorgeous Edwardian and Victorian buildings in the town centre. The city was elegant in its beauty. Luscious, green gardens extended throughout the city, and the trees stood naked and proud in the face of the cold. Small shops lined the roads, and the quiet buzz of people and cars drifted on the breeze. Before long, I embraced the remote and isolated Dunedin, so different from the bustling, populated cities of India, and quieter and more tranquil compared to Auckland.

Now that I had a stable and comfortable job, I arranged for my wife Sandhya to fly to Dunedin from India. She joined me within a week of my arrival, and like me, she initially struggled from culture shock, but soon felt at home. The newness and natural beauty were refreshing, and we thrived in our new freedom from the expectations of friends and family. The roads and the streets dipped and rolled with the mountainous terrain, and the view from our house over the tree-lined landscape was breathtaking.

I enjoyed my new role, too. I had everything I ever dreamed of in my job. Initially, it was challenging to communicate with my clients because of my thick accent. Still, I put in lots of late hours at work, and my hiring manager, Amanda Cameron, supported me completely. She was a great leader and I admired her leadership skills. I was fortunate to work with her and it was a great learning experience. I made sure my clients, who were mostly university researchers, were well looked after. Life went on smoothly for almost three years. We settled down and made a lovely home for ourselves.

In the new millennium, we were blessed with a baby girl, and I was thrust into the lifelong adventure of fatherhood. A couple of years later, just as my wife and I had gotten used to dealing with our energetic and stubborn daughter, Sanjana, we were granted another reckless bundle of energy in the form of a wide-eyed baby boy, Sanjit.

A couple of months after our son's Sanjit's birth, we decided to relocate to Perth, Australia. Being in Australia was a real transition for us after living in New Zealand for over seven years. Perth was much warmer, and the temperatures in summer soared, except when the 'Fremantle doctor' or the 'Freo doctor', a term that was used in Perth for the cooling afternoon sea breeze, came to our rescue. We didn't know anyone, and it took a few months to fall into a rhythm. But soon, we settled down in our new home. Life was good.

Seven

Realisation of Mortality

When the veil lifts, we see small miracles and fresh
perspective everywhere.

Quite abruptly, I suffered from persistent, excruciating back pain that spread towards my chest. I tried everything to soothe my afflicted body. I corrected my posture and used a better pillow for sleeping. I also did exercises under the guidance of a physical therapist. None of my efforts helped, and the piercing pain persisted.

One summer night, the pain was so severe that I got out of bed and paced around the living room, praying for relief. I felt something in my chest blocking my airways, so I went to the bathroom to clear my throat. I kept coughing, and my lungs burned with the effort. When I looked down, I saw blood along with phlegm. Having had a father who smoked, I knew this wasn't a good sign. However, I wasn't a smoker or even a drinker. As far as I knew, I was healthy and fit. But as I tried to sleep, my mind stirred. I worried about what was going on in my body before finally falling into a restless sleep. When I woke up, I booked an appointment with my doctor.

He listened to my symptoms and the previous night's events and asked questions about my smoking and alcohol habits, to which I replied that I used neither. The doctor ordered lung X-rays, which I undertook that same day before going to work in the afternoon, still struggling with the chest pain.

When the alarm rang the next morning, I groaned and shuffled my way out of bed. I had hardly slept, waking up multiple times, pacing around the room, and trying physio exercises. I got ready for work as usual and was just about to enter my office when I got an urgent call from the hospital asking me to come quickly. My heart pounded in my chest and sweat beaded on my forehead. Somehow, I managed to stay calm and drive to the hospital.

When I got to the doctor's office, he smiled. But the warmth didn't quite reach his eyes. Something was wrong, and we both knew it. He explained that the X-ray from the previous day showed something unusual, and he would like to run a few tests and suggested an immediate scan. Shocked, I nodded my head and followed the nurse as she led me away for the scan. The whole episode felt surreal. *Am I dreaming?* I thought. *Sleepwalking?*

Following the scan, I sat in the waiting area, and when he called me in, I knew by the look on his face that something was seriously wrong. I gripped the sides of the chair.

'I have some bad news for you,' he said. 'There is a mass in your lungs, and the results of the scan indicate you have an advanced stage of lung cancer.'

I could only stare at him. My mind went blank. Everything stopped. The doctor called out my name, trying to get my attention, but I continued to stare into space. I could hear his words but was unable to comprehend them.

'I can recommend a well-recognised and respected oncologist. I suggest you consult him straight away. I don't mean to alarm you; however, I suspect you may have to go under the knife straight away.'

I nodded blankly. My heart hammered in my chest, threatening to erupt. The doctor looked at me sympathetically, then picked up the phone to call the oncologist. I listened to the words being spoken, still in a daze. All I could think about was, *What will happen? How will I tell my wife? My family?* All these thoughts bombarded me. It was the single most frightening moment of my life—not knowing what would happen and having no control over the situation.

The doctor booked an appointment with the oncologist for that evening, giving me time to break the news to my wife. Feeling numb, I walked out of the room past the doctor, who patted me on the shoulder. Somehow, I drove home, although I have no recollection of it.

I walked into the house to the sound of a crying baby and a singing toddler. Ignoring everything, I collapsed on the couch, cradling my pounding head in my hands. My daughter came and shook my hands, trying to reveal my face. She probably thought it was a game.

My wife came in, carrying our sleeping baby. She took one look at me and asked what was wrong. I explained the whole thing, and she listened, showing no expression, just stunned silence. My son woke, but she just sat there staring down at him. She finally came back to conscious awareness and cradled the baby, soothing him back to sleep. As she rocked him, she placed a warm hand over my own. 'It'll be alright. I'm here for you and we'll do everything we can to get through this,' she said. Although I knew she was scared, she put on a facade of strength.

That evening, we drove to the specialist centre with our two sleeping children in the back. We were silent the whole journey, broken only by the soft breathing of the children. As we waited to see the oncologist, my hands would not stop shaking. My wife sat in the chair beside me, rocking our sleeping son in her arms. Without realising it, he was giving her comfort.

When the oncologist called my name, we followed him into the examination room. He was the type of person who makes people feel at ease in his presence. He had a calm tone of voice and made small talk with us, laughing and joking about children and the weather in Perth.

He must have noticed our anxiousness because he spoke honestly about my condition. When he talked about my scan, his voice turned sombre, and we knew bad news was about to strike.

'After looking at your scans and talking with Dr Ryan, I suspect you are in the advanced stages of lung cancer,' he said. 'Based on my years of experience, I recommend that you undergo surgery to remove the mass in your lungs.'

Like Dr Ryan, the oncologist was patient and sympathetic. He also suggested an endoscopy and dye test before the biopsy to ensure that all precautions were considered. This was to be done as soon as possible so a date for the surgery could be finalised.

He was patient in explaining other tests that could also confirm cancer, in addition to the biopsy. He also said there was a waiting list for the procedure. I looked at my wife, hundreds of questions buzzing through my head: *How long will the surgery take? What's the chance of survival after the surgery? How long do I have to live?* The latter—the most pressing question—had been ringing inside my head since I first found out about the diagnosis.

Finally, I could not hold on to it anymore. 'How long do I have to live?' I said, interrupting the doctor.

He seemed shocked by my outburst, but he quickly regained composure, his face taking on a grim expression. My heart raced as I waited for his answer. He spoke slowly, 'It is always difficult to be certain, especially as we don't know the nature of the tumour. The biopsy has not been conducted yet, and the potential results are different for different people, especially based on severity and symptoms.' He paused, considering me. My eyes never left his face—I think he realised I was expecting a more definite answer. He took a deep breath. 'From my years of experience in cases like these, it is likely you have a maximum of between six months to two years.'

It was like someone kicked me in the stomach. I stopped breathing. I stopped feeling. I felt utterly lost. Tears streamed down my face, and my body shook silently. The doctor stopped talking and looked at us with genuine sorrow. It must be an emotionally demanding job, telling families and patients they don't have much time left.

'I'll give you a few minutes to process the news,' said the oncologist.

Tears streamed down my wife's face. Her knuckles had gone white from gripping the sides of the chair. She turned to me, her eyes full of despair. It was heartbreaking. I looked at my children, still sleeping soundlessly in the pram. So young, so innocent. They didn't know their lives were about to change forever. Sorrow struck me when I realised I wouldn't see them grow up. Soon I wouldn't be alive to spend time with my family or embrace my children. In those few minutes, I felt as though everything had been taken from me. My life was ending prematurely, and it would affect the lives of my wife and children. I wasn't worried about myself, but the vulnerable family I would leave behind. We had no friends or family in Australia. They would have no support once I was gone.

I felt so helpless and alone.

That night I was awake until morning, sitting on the sofa and staring out of the window, watching the darkness of the night. My mind was agitated as I tried to figure out a solution to why I had cancer. I couldn't accept the diagnosis. *How can a person who never smoked or drank and who exercised nearly every day get cancer? Why did this happen to me? Why do I have to suffer? How will I tell my family? My parents, my sister, brother and in-laws?*

I couldn't even admit it to myself, let alone to all the people I loved and who loved me. It didn't seem fair. There was so much more to achieve in life and so much more to experience.

*   *   *

The next morning, I decided there was no point in putting it off any longer. I called my parents and in-laws and told them. The response from both calls was the same: pure shock. I had never told them about my back pain, so it was a significant blow. My parents were with my sister in Sacramento, California, for her first child's birth, and they offered as much emotional support as they could. When my in-laws heard about it, they offered to come immediately. We needed the help. My wife wouldn't be able to deal with the emotional toll of the diagnosis and take care of everything else. I also called my employer and my manager John Johnstone to explain the situation. John was sympathetic and gave me time to take care of myself and my family.

The day of the biopsy finally arrived. It was daunting knowing it would be the most influential test of my life. When I think back to all the tests I stressed about during my academic life, it makes me laugh at how naïve I was. It seemed ironic that I was about to take a test that would determine my survival, while for all those years, I worried about grades and tests and academic achievements.

*   *   *

My in-laws hadn't arrived yet, so my wife and children drove with me to the hospital. My daughter kept asking where we were going, but neither of us wanted to answer her innocent question. When we reached the hospital, I parked the car. However, I couldn't conjure up the courage to get out. My hands shook, and my skin felt hot and clammy. I stared out the car window, trying to regain composure, even as every cell in my body was screaming in distress.

My wife turned to look at me, but I couldn't look at her. She would see the fear in my eyes.

She carefully placed her hand on mine, and the warmth and energy in her touch woke me from my dazed state. 'Everything will be okay,' she said softly. As always, her strength and courage supported me. My whole life, I faced challenges and overcame them. The only thing I could do now was face my situation.

Walking into the Fremantle hospital in Perth, I knew I was at a turning point—the fate of my life and the lives of my family depended on this one test. I got down on my knees to hug my daughter. Then I took my son from my wife's arms and cuddled him to me, his tiny head resting on my shoulder. Although I always valued these moments with my family, after my cancer diagnosis, I cherished them. It was another moment I could have with them, a moment that could soon be no more. I handed my son back to my wife and kissed her gently on the forehead. Keeping a brave face, I walked towards the surgery waiting room. They would wait for me outside throughout the whole procedure. My wife said later that she prayed for hours in the hospital chapel.

She explained that, miraculously, the children slept the entire time, never once making a sound.

As I lay on a gurney being wheeled into surgery, I contemplated the transient nature of life. *Why do we spend our time struggling and dissatisfied when our existence on earth is so short?* Within a few minutes, I was lying face down on the operating table. I couldn't see the doctors around me, but I heard them talking and concentrating their attention on my back. A pathologist stood beside the surgeon waiting for the tissue sample that would determine my fate.

It was a weird experience. Throughout the procedure, I felt like an outsider watching everything. I felt only faint sensations as they inserted the large needle into a small incision into my chest from the back of my body to extract some tissue. But then an excruciating pain arose in my chest and surged throughout my body. I shook from the force of it and groaned in agony. Every cell of my body vibrated from the pain. I felt as though I had been shocked, and death was already overtaking me.

But as suddenly as the piercing pain started, it dissipated, and a feeling of peace came over me. I lay on the surgery table, helpless and ultimately resigned to what was going on around me. But for some reason, I felt as though I was no longer a part of my body, and I was watching the whole scene from somewhere else. I accepted it all: the surgery, the cancer diagnosis, and even the prospect of death. There was nothing I could do. I had no power, no control. At that moment, I felt completely liberated. My body buzzed with energy and life. Although I was so close to death, I had never felt so alive.

Unexpectedly, a soothing, gentle voice whispered in my ear, 'You're going to be fine. You don't have cancer.' I opened my eyes and looked up at a face silhouetted by bright golden light. I squinted to see it more clearly, but the origin of the reassuring voice had disappeared. Within minutes, I felt myself being pulled into darkness as my body willingly fell into the quiet realm of sleep.

I stirred, confused about where I was. Opening my heavy eyelids, I squinted at the bright light streaming out of the open windows. I blinked a couple of times, allowing my pupils to adjust to the light. My wife rushed over to my side and looked down at me with concern. I smiled at her, grateful to see her again.

I felt like I was seeing her for the first time. I noticed every detail: the curve and hollows of her beautiful face, the glimmer of hope and courage in her eyes, the strength of character in her expression, as well as the love she held for her family. I looked down at my daughter, and it was like seeing her for the first time, too. She had changed so dramatically since she was born. Her button features had developed, and I could see her mother's eyes and nose in her round face. Her eyes held a determined and curious expression, depicting her stubborn and independent character.

When I turned to look at my baby boy, I noticed his massive brown eyes were the exact same shade as my father's eyes. It was the most astonishing thing—all these years, I had been blind and now I had been gifted with sight. Everything was new and beautiful.

My wife was excited to tell me I didn't have cancer. I nodded in relief, and I told her about hearing the reassuring voice. She looked at me in astonishment. She explained that while she was sitting in the chapel waiting for news about the surgery, a soft voice had whispered the same message to her. When she turned around, she had seen a petite nurse with blonde hair smiling down at her. When my wife jumped up and embraced the nurse, the nurse hugged her back, gently encouraging her and providing strength.

Later, when we inquired about the angelic nurse to thank her, we learned she had disappeared, and no one had any information about her—almost as though her purpose was to convey the good news to us and help us. It seemed like a miracle.

During times of dire anguish—when we have lost all hope, and our prospects are bleak—a tender, caring hand, and a voice so loving, can appear, leaving us so mesmerised that we are brought back from the brink of collapse. They come when you need them most and then disappear, even before you can regain your senses. We may often dismiss such serendipitous experiences as sheer luck or coincidence, but, in truth, they are something more.

Eight

On the Bright Side of Life

Becoming aware of the silence.

I walked out of the revolving hospital doors feeling as though I had escaped from prison. After months of treatment for a serious infection in my lungs, the doctors had confirmed that I was medically healthy and no longer needed further treatment. It was like waking up from a deep slumber. My body was alive, and I was acutely aware of the beautiful world around me. I walked towards the parking lot with my family, breathing deeply and allowing the fresh air to fill my lungs. I closed my eyes for a moment, and when I opened them, I was no longer merely *looking*. I was *seeing*. Seeing the world around me with full awareness; strokes of golden light radiated across the vast blue sky, flowers danced in the cool breeze, bees hovered over the soft grass carpeting the hospital grounds, and the walkways were lined with trees in the process of changing from green to shades of gold and auburn.

I was suddenly aware of the silence in my head—I was no

longer bombarded by my thoughts. Instead, I became aware of a different kind of sound that seemed to occur in a rhythm, coming together in a beautiful, synchronised song. The whispering of the leaves and the slow hum of moving cars fell into unison. The rumble of a train faded as it passed by into the distance. I felt a sense of awareness beyond anything I had ever experienced before. I felt utterly alive, as if I had gained a new lease on life, which, in fact, I had. This was my second birth, an opportunity to start anew and discover my true purpose.

I experienced a newfound purpose and embraced life. There was no urgency to acquire or achieve; I was content with all that I had. Material things seemed so trivial in comparison to the beauty of life. Pure joy emanated from within me.

I was eager to wake up in the morning, and some days I woke up as early as four o'clock. Sitting quietly as the sun came up, I would immerse myself in the quietness, waiting eagerly for the sounds of the early birds singing. Bright orange beams of light would filter through the curtains, illuminating the dark room in hues of gold and pink.

I began to enjoy the presence of nature. Morning walks became an everyday ritual. The cool morning breeze caressed the leaves and I embraced each step, listening and tuning into each moment. I was fully conscious of everything around me—the tiny ants carrying morsels of food, the grasshopper quenching its thirst with the early morning dew, the butterflies teasing the brightly coloured flowers, and the grass bending with the weight of the dew.

I was at peace with time, no longer blindfolded and missing out on the life around me. The blindfold of limited intellect had been lifted, and I was mesmerised by the vibrancy of nature. I had stepped off the fast-paced treadmill of my life and was suddenly aware of the abundance of time I had, to continue living. The incessant thoughts that usually inundated my head were silenced. There was no persistent voice resonating within my brain, demanding me to get things done. I no longer worried about work and rushing home. I was no longer burdened by deadlines or time restraints.

What happened? Why this new awareness of myself and everything around me? Why do I feel so alive? Did my close encounter with mortality bring about this awareness? Thoughts and feelings that were once unconscious processes could now be consciously stalled. But I felt unable to convey these new revelations to others. I didn't know how to express what was a very personal experience. I was worried about what people would think of my rapid transformation. They might label it 'spiritual' or 'religious'. So, I kept these experiences to myself. Nevertheless, I was intrigued by this new state of being and keen to understand it, although I had no idea where to begin and wondered: *Is this what people mean when they talk about self-discovery?*

Nine

State of Mind

*Is there a relationship between continuous compulsive
thinking and our mental state of being?*

The relationship between the intellect and how we feel about
life is intriguing. The incessant thought-patterns remaining
from the first part of my life were overwhelming. My life used to
be a state of continual acting and reacting without ever genuinely
living in the moment. I didn't even realise there was more to life
than the fast-paced and disillusioned way of life that I previously
led. I didn't know my anxious state of mind was preventable. I
always assumed that anxiety and constant mind chatter were
normal—something that we must learn to cope with.

Now, when I think back to my old life, I wonder why I was so
stressed. I had no control over my emotions; a single thought
could produce such a strong response in me.

*   *   *

Memories from my past stirred within me, transporting me back to the paddy fields of Kannur in Kerala. Playing with my friends, swimming in the cool river and chasing after large, darting fish, or climbing the strong branches of the mango trees and tasting the sweet, juicy flesh of the golden fruit. But now, the large ancestral homes were likely demolished, buried with their history and memories, the families migrated away to distant cities. All these memories came flooding back, taking me to a previous world and abducting me from the present.

Sometimes, I thought of the time I spent with my grandfather, who passed away when I was very young. Gone were the times when he held my hand as we walked together across the paddy fields, my short legs hastening to catch up with his long strides. The quiet days when we went to the small street tea shop in the neighbouring village and sat on the wooden benches, enjoying our steaming tea as the sun set in the distance. As I thought of our time together and the fact that I could no longer look at his wise face or drink tea with him, I felt an aching sadness. Though he was gone, the memory still managed to trigger despair within me.

Then there were thoughts of the future, driven by my insatiable ambition and desire for a high-flying job, to make a name for myself and prove myself to others, to compete against others and get that number one spot.

These obsessive thoughts about my past and potential future created anxiety and fear, which contributed to my feelings of incompleteness and disillusionment. I wondered: *Is there a relationship between continuous compulsive thinking and our mental state of being?*

Ten

The Vital Question:

Beginning to answer, 'Who am I?'

We visited my parents in India every other year, usually during December and January, summertime in Australia. They always looked forward to our visits and seeing their grandchildren. One afternoon, Dad and I were sitting across from each other. He was reading a book while I typed an email on my laptop. Sighing, he put down his book, 'Santosh, when are you coming back to India?'

I stared at him. *Come back to India? When has that even been an option?* 'Umm ... well ...,' I said tentatively. 'I wasn't planning on returning anytime soon. Especially with our work and the children's school.' My dad looked at me for a few moments, his face strained. 'Dad, you know I'm quite happy in Australia. It's my home.'

He looked away, tapping his hands on the book cover. Noticing the shift in mood, I closed my laptop and waited for him to respond. His disappointment was palpable, and I squirmed, feeling like a

67

young kid again. *Get a grip. You're now forty-two years old. You don't have to be scared anymore. You can make your own choices.*

'Santosh, I never understood your ambition to leave India. I still don't. And when you began to be independent and explore, your mother and I were immensely proud of you. But I had hoped that it was all a phase, a phase where you wanted to explore, to travel. You can't honestly think of staying there for years longer. Think about your health! Have you forgotten what happened? You need the support of your family. You should come home.'

I understood my father's concern but having been away from India for more than ten years, I wasn't ready to go back. I wanted to stay in Australia. The conversation got more heated, eventually turning into a full-blown argument. Neither of us was listening to each other. I tried to defend my reasoning for remaining in Australia while he tried to reason with my supposed immaturity.

Just as the argument intensified, my father got up and walked away, leaving me standing there conflicted and fuming. I walked to my bedroom and slammed the door. My head buzzed, like I was fighting an imaginary battle.

In my mind, I was rationalising my own decisions, with no desire to change my stance. As my anger subsided, I realised that the conversation had been unnecessarily conflicted. If only I had spoken my mind and been more patient, I could have had a better conversation with my father. I almost felt guilty for the way I handled it. Almost.

I sat on the edge of my bed, elbows resting on my knees and face in my hands. Guilt, embarrassment, regret, frustration, and sadness bubbled within me. Why was everything so hard? I sat there, palms pressed against my forehead, hoping that the pressure would ease away the pain and confusion. I wanted to be a good son, someone my father could trust and respect, but I had just proved the complete opposite. I regretted not controlling my anger and ego; I lost control of myself when talking to him. My anger-fuelled words echoed in my head, and I felt genuine regret and sadness. He didn't deserve my anger. He had the right to be concerned. He had the right to want his son to be close to him, especially as he got older. I was sorry for the words that I said to him. I knew they hurt; I knew it wasn't me, but at the time, I wanted to say them. I wanted to hurt him. I wanted the monster inside to feed off his hurt and fuel my anger.

I could have easily gone to apologise. I may not have been able to take back my words, but I could have let my dad know how wrong I was to have said them. But something inside me stirred. I couldn't make myself get up. I couldn't apologise. The voice in my head argued, riling the anger and frustration towards my father. *Why do I have to apologise? Why does he still treat me like a child? He's the father. He should be a mature adult in this situation. Why doesn't he even try to think from my point of view? He's so inconsiderate. No! Don't apologise. Don't belittle yourself.*

I sat there, intently listening to this voice when suddenly I questioned it. *Whose voice is that? Where did it come from? Why is a voice in my head ruining my relationship with my father? This is the same voice that has driven me to get angry in the first place, goading me on, driving me to say horrible things to my father. It is manipulative.*

Hasn't it already done enough damage? It is dangerous. And it isn't me. I sat up confused. *How can one part of me be so apologetic and compassionate, and the other be so brutally arrogant? If so, which one am I? Who am I?*

Suddenly, almost like some spark in my brain was triggered, I remembered the same question posed to me by someone else. It was like travelling back in time. The old hall. The crowd. The guru. My question. Then the guru. 'The question to which you must first find an answer, and probably one of the hardest questions of all is, "Who am I? Who am I really? Ponder over it".'

Who am I really? The demonic voice in my head or the forgiving, innocent one.

*   *   *

'Who am I? What am I?' Saying it aloud made no difference. I was just as clueless to the answer as I had been when I was twelve years old.

Who am I? The question popped into my head so abruptly, it was almost like a voice had whispered it in my ear. I sat up. *Okay, so this one I might be able to answer. Who am I? Who have I been?* I wrote it down in my leatherbound journal, hoping it would give me clarity. *Santosh. An arrogant, conceited prick, driven by insatiable ambition.* Nodding to myself in satisfaction, I wrote it down. *Okay, what else? I was incredibly angry and stressed all the time. God knows what for, but yes, I was. Very jealous of almost* everyone. *I wanted everything that others had. The name, fame, power, and especially money. Bad man.*

Looking down at the page of negatives, I felt myself deflating. *Wow, this is rough—but aren't a lot of people like this?* Angry, envious, ambitious, stressed, and anxious. I see it in the faces of so many people all the time. Just go to the city on any weekday morning. Hundreds of serious faces set into determined expressions of indifference as they march across the concrete footpath to their dreaded destinations. Everyone has their issues, their problems. We all have strong emotions that we can't control. We have opinions, judgements. We express envy, jealousy, hatred, and violence when instigated. Society is filled with negativity and violence. Human beings kill each other; families, friends, and colleagues fight and dispute when a disagreement arises.

But if this is normal for human beings, does that mean it is right? Is this the only way that we can survive in this world? Moments of happiness with several intermittent episodes of anger, sadness, jealousy, envy, and anger? Are we meant to be spending most of our lives struggling? Why are we not at ease with ourselves or our lives? Why must we continue to struggle? It was the first time I had ever questioned anything in my life. Until then, I had acquiesced to every rule and instruction that was thrown at me. With this one question, everything that I had been taught throughout my forty years of existence was unravelling. Everything could be a massive illusion. *So, what is the truth?*

I decided to do something I had never done: to observe and study myself. It was almost ironic how in all these years, I looked towards others to guide me. I never once made a decision that was purely mine and never tried to understand myself. I looked at my emotions—my fear, anger, anxiety, and greed. I observed the emotions and the conditioned behaviours that prevented me from fully flowering in life. These were the same emotions that had created a barrier between me and those around me. My rage could destroy relationships, fuelling me into saying things I never would have said otherwise. My greed spurred me to selfishly climb up the ladder, stepping on many helping hands on the way up. I had become ruthless in my single-minded pursuit of success. My fear was tethered to me, gripping me, and growing like a poisonous weed, trapping me in its tendrils.

Throughout my life, fear had also been a stumbling block. I would take one step forwards, and my fear of failing or rejection would force me two steps backwards. I didn't dare to embrace life fully, to do what I wanted, or even try something new. I was always inhibited by the fear of failure, fear of proving to myself that I am, in fact, that worthless person I had always tried to hide.

I was constantly living a life of stress. I was always anxious about the future. What if? What if not? Anxious about things that I couldn't control. My body and mind were in a constant state of anxiety, worried about things that may or may not eventuate. It was exhausting. My insecurity shadowed me in darkness, blinding me, inhibiting me from leaving my cage.

The continued belief of my poor command of English often left me with an intense fear that I wouldn't be able to articulate to my colleagues and friends. I worried that they would look at me in contempt when they realised I was illiterate, almost like a shadow of my memory from my childhood. I was living in a self-imposed cage. It had a debilitating effect throughout my life. I lived most of my life trying to prove to others that I was worthy. But I never once believed it. I didn't respect or trust myself. It was the worst form of self-inflicted torture.

I hoped that if I realised the root cause of all my emotions, then maybe I would be able to let them go and finally be free. It seemed ridiculous, even to me; to relieve myself of emotions was almost like trying to run away from my own shadow—futile and tiring.

Nevertheless, something inside me burned—the flicker of a flame that I had when I was a child fighting for equality for my friends. Now, the fire was still burning. My priorities had realigned, and I finally had the time, urgency, and desire to discover the root cause of it all—the truth.

Eleven

Getting to the root cause

Seeing the light at the end of the tunnel.

O ne winter morning, I walked along a trail near my house, shivering from the cold wind. Pulling my scarf tightly around my neck and stuffing my hands into my pockets, I followed my daughter, who was skipping with boundless energy in front of me. When she stopped near the shallow lake to play with the leaves, I took a seat behind her on a wooden bench and sat huddling into my jacket. I sighed, the air puffing in front of me. Sitting back against the hard wood, I watched her playing with a stick and collecting the floating leaves from the surface of the lake, almost like fishing, for leaves. I shook my head in amusement and let myself admire the view. The sky was overcast, the thick dark clouds blanketing the city in a shadowed haze. The lake reflected the dull grey colour of the sky and rippled in the cold wind. On the other side of the lake, a tall, regal tree stood bare, its long branches extending out on both sides from the dark, robust body of the tree, almost like a person with their arms outstretched. I found myself staring at the tree—the branches extending from the body, and its roots deep into the earth, feeding and nourishing its growth.

When I got home, my daughter rushed inside to show her mother her collection of soggy leaves as I went into my study. I opened my leatherbound journal to a new page and wrote down each of my debilitating emotions—fear, anger, jealousy, ambition, selfishness, lack of confidence, loneliness. Each word was scattered around the upper half of the page, floating on the white sheet. As I put all these words down one by one, in my mind, it formed a pattern on the white sheet of paper. It looked like the branches of a tree. My immediate reaction was to draw a tree with each branch depicting my emotions. My fingers easily sketched out the lines, bringing the branches together to form the tree's body, and beneath the tree, much like the one near the lake, I drew winding deep roots. The roots nurtured and supported the growth of the branches.

I leaned back, exhilarated. *This is it! This is what I need to find— the root cause! If I just prune the branches and control my emotions, they will still thrive and grow.* I needed to discover the root cause and stop the growth of this dangerous tree within me before it grew out of my control.

*   *   *

As I attempted to continue my self-discovery towards truth, I felt overwhelmed by the complexity and the vast amount of knowledge and questioning that was occurring within me. Over the past couple of weeks, I had perused the bookshelves in the local library and bought many self-help books. I studied each book and analysed the content—books on meditation, finding inner peace, spirituality, inner growth and motivation. I listened to CDs and watched videos of authors, spiritual teachers, and speakers sharing the purpose of life. As I embraced each new piece of information, each quote, I could feel myself falling deeper into a hole. There was so much. Too much. I felt inundated by all the advice, from all the information. Like a boiling pot threatening to bubble and spill over, I could feel myself beginning to lose everything I had learned from the confusion of all this new knowledge.

Putting my latest book down, I leaned back into my chair. My neck and shoulders were cramped. I rolled my shoulders to release the tension. Placing my sock-clad feet onto my desk, I tried to relax. At that moment, my foot pushed my laptop, which pushed something off my desk. I picked up my leatherbound book, which opened to my unfinished tree. The rough sketch of the bare tree with wide arching branches stood out against the starkness of the white paper.

Over the last few weeks, I recognised that each of the branches represented more than just my emotions. But, in fact, all my conditioning—my anger, my fear, and other emotions, including ambition and its associated transient happiness. Still, I had also added my arrogance, my ego, my likes, my dislikes, my attachments, my fear, my anxiety, my hurt, my opinions, my countless memories, and all the baggage associated with my life. However, the root cause that nurtures all these branches was still unknown.

I was sitting at my desk, typing out something for work, when my daughter bounded into the room. She skipped up beside me and paused, watching me, and then looked around. 'Dad ... I was thinking ...' she said slowly.

'What were you thinking?' I asked, humouring her while still staring at my computer screen, trying to remember what I was typing.

'I was *thinking* ... oh, is that a tree?' Perplexed, I looked at the tree I had drawn. 'It's not very good, Dad.'

I laughed. 'Well, we can't all be as good as you, can we?' She nodded, nonplussed. I looked down at my tree. 'Anyway, what were you thinking?'

'Oh, umm ... oh yeah, I *thought* that maybe I could have some ice-cream before dinner because I'm hungry,' she tested innocently.

My brain stopped listening. Thinking ... thoughts ... My brain blanked, and for just a moment, I felt something click into place. *Is that it? Is that part of the answer?*

As I thought about it, it made complete sense. All my previous experiences were recorded away in my brain in the form of memories. Every single moment is remembered, from my very first memory as a two-year-old toddling in my backyard to this very moment. We constantly go back and retrieve all these experiences, be it fear, anger, anxiety, happiness, and project them into the future, making us feel angry, hurt, fearful, anxious, or even happy. We have immense storage for all our memories within the brain, all of which influence our present as well as our future. So, thoughts move back and forth like a pendulum, retrieving PAST experiences of fear and anger, for example, and projecting these experiences and memories into the FUTURE.

'Dad! So, can I?'

I was shaken out of my reverie by someone tugging at my arm. I looked down at my daughter, who stared at me curiously. 'Why don't you go ask your mum?' I said patiently.

She didn't seem very happy and pouted her mouth. 'Fine,' she said as she walked off. In an almost whisper, I heard her mutter to herself as she left, 'But, she already said no!'

Shaking my head at her cunningness, I turned back to my book and allowed my train of discovery to continue.

This is why we often feel a great deal of anxiety. Incessant and constant thoughts in our minds can be so tiring, leading to situations where we constantly feel stressed or anxious.

I felt my scientific mind firing up as I delved deeper. Every thought in our head sends a message to our brains, signalling each of the ten trillion cells within our body and back through a highly specialised network of neurons. These thoughts in our head are generally about the past or the future. If our thoughts concern a past incident of our life, we may be initiating a cascade of fear, anger, hatred, envy, or even happiness, to each of the ten trillion cells and back. If the thoughts concern the future, we may be sending a signal of anxiety. Either way, our cells are constantly under the pump, reacting to various signals from the brain. Our emotions are reactions to our thoughts. This inevitably results in each of the cells correspondingly reacting to what we think. When we are angry, our cells also feel the wrath and tension of our anger. Likewise, when we are worried about something, each of our cells feels anxiety. Thus, the incessant thought movement can be potentially harmful to our physical bodies. *But how much longer can our cells survive in these stressed conditions?* Sooner or later, the cells will start to retaliate, and you may end up with a condition called disease.

Hence our cells, our entire bodies, are not at ease with the constant barrage of signals from the brain. As a result, our body may succumb to diseases as it cannot withstand the external pressures that we inflict upon it. If there is incessant thought activity, anxiety and stress will always exist in our life. This is what causes us so much strife in our lives.

It made so much sense. Our thought activity seems to be the main source of anxiety, and this is instigated through our memories. However, we all seem to be completely unaware of this thought activity happening within us because we have become accustomed to living this way. Yet if this is the case, with that kind of thought activity—or shall we say, mind noise—in our heads, how can we read a book, like this one in your hand currently, with 'undivided' attention? How can we listen to what others are saying or truly see the world outside of ourselves? So, it becomes like a parallel world. We live within our thoughts on the inside, while the world outside passes without us even noticing it.

Every moment of our existence, we are engaged in acting on and reacting to thoughts. And every thought tells us, 'I am important, so you better take care of me; otherwise, you'll get into trouble.' And so, these thoughts keep us on a constant treadmill, and we continue to act and react to each one. Each thought vies for our attention. We are, therefore, generally anxious, stressed, living in fear and anger, with transient moments of happiness in between. As a result, we seldom see, hear, or listen to anything happening on the outside—or rather, we only have partial attention to things outside of ourselves. As such, we fail to see the beauty of nature contained within the external world—flowers blooming, birds singing, and the spectacle of nature dancing before us. Instead, all go unnoticed—all due to the incessant thought activity in our heads.

I knew there had to be another way. *What if I don't go back into the past stored memory to retrieve and project into the future?* Logically, it would mean not accessing any of my past experiences. If I didn't access any of my past experiences, my mind wouldn't constantly be wandering. I would remain in the present moment—in the now. My past would not affect my present. All the baggage would remain in my memory, but I merely don't access it. It's only when I allow my mind to take control and let it go back and access my memories of fear or anger that it affects me in the present. Therefore, the incessant thinking or our thoughts must be the root cause of all our fear, anger, anxiety, the stress in our lives!

I also recognised how there are certain memories that we

require to function in this manifested society. For example, we need to know our names, the way back to our home, and so on. Therefore, some memory is useful; otherwise, life would be dysfunctional. We have learned certain basic things in physics, chemistry, engineering, for example. Those memories are required. Otherwise, we would not have development and intellectual growth would be impossible.

It's not our memories or thoughts that are the root cause of our problems. It's our lack of awareness. Our default is to go back into the memory to retrieve old memories, feelings, and emotions, which are relayed as thoughts. Unfortunately, these conditioned thoughts influence the way we perceive the world. When bad experiences and memories stay with us, they significantly corrupt our present. The problem is we are unaware of what we are thinking. Therefore, by default, we go back and retrieve the past baggage, affecting the present moment and inevitably, the future. *But what if we are fully conscious or mindful? Would we knowingly go back and retrieve all the unwanted and bad experiences stored in our brain?* Those memories will, therefore, continue to remain in our brain; however, we could choose not to access them. Hence, the root cause of most of our struggle is our lack of self-awareness. We allow our minds to overwhelm us, trigger our emotions, and completely take over. We're struggling because we have no control over our lives. It's honestly like all this time we are navigating the world blindfolded, and until we gain awareness, we are blind and stumbling through the complex maze, completely lost and directionless. We seem to have control of our body parts, like our hands and legs. *However, we don't have control of our minds. Isn't that ironic?*

I sighed. It made so much sense. I had no idea how, but it did. Nothing had ever felt so true, so profoundly freeing. But this one question was gnawing at the back of my mind. *If we are so conditioned by our thoughts and become trapped, where did it all go wrong? When did it all go wrong? When and where did we take a wrong turn in life?*

Twelve

The Joy of Innocence

Inheriting a roadmap doesn't
necessarily lead to happiness.

E xhausted from shopping, I sat on a plush couch in the middle of the shopping centre in Chadstone in the south-eastern suburbs of Melbourne, watching the harried shoppers walk past, catching snippets of conversations. The whole building buzzed with energy as people rushed to finish their Christmas shopping. Tinsel, fairy lights, and lit trees adorned every corner of the massive shopping centre; colours and lights reflecting off the shiny windows. Looking into the store in front of me, my wife peered at items while my daughter dutifully followed. My son ran through the racks, hiding in between clothes. I leaned back into the seat, straightening my tired legs. Closing my eyes for a moment, I attempted to meditate, hoping that it would calm my mind. I sat there, listening to the noises around me and allowing myself to relax. Placing attention to my mind, I observed its movement, noticing when it became distracting.

'Excuse me, may I use this seat?'

I opened my eyes to see a woman with a stroller pointing at the seat beside me. 'Of course,' I replied. Closing my eyes once more, I became immersed in my senses as I attempted to stay in the present moment. When I finally opened my eyes, I was met by the face of a baby. His wide brown eyes stared at me as he cocked his head to one side, almost like he was studying me. The woman was frantically searching through her carrier bags. When she finally found her phone, she leaned back in relief and began scrolling through it. Her baby continued to watch me, so I smiled at him, giving him a little wave. He gurgled and kicked his little legs against the stroller. His mother looked up and smiled at me. 'How old is he?' I asked.

'Eight months,' she said. 'It's his first Christmas.' The baby beamed as if realising that we were talking about him and waved his fisted arms towards me. Leaning forwards, I held his little hand, like a little handshake.

'What's your name, little guy?'

Kicking his little legs, he gurgled. 'Aetos,' his mother answered. 'It was my grandfather's name. My husband really liked it. I guess he thought it sounded unique.'

At that moment, my phone rang. 'Sorry, excuse me.' Guessing that it was my wife, I looked towards the store to see that they were standing outside looking for me. 'That's my cue to get back. It was nice meeting you both. And I hope you both have a good Christmas.' The woman smiled, and I waved at the baby. Smiling at his adorable, glowing face, I walked off towards my own children, who were peering through the glass balustrade to the level below.

*   *   *

As I drove home, I thought about how children are enthused about everything and how we change as we grow up. When we are born, we possess a natural abundance of happiness. Our brains are fresh and pure. We are one with the world, full of vitality and beauty. We are full of joy and observe the world with awe and wonderment. However, around the age of two or three, we understand that we are separate from other people and our surroundings. How does this happen?

As young children, we continue to rely on our parents, teachers, and the rest of society to instruct us on what to say and do. They tell us what is good for us, which school to attend, what clothes to wear, and how to behave. We quickly learn that to survive, we must conform to whatever our parents, teachers, and other adults say, or risk being labelled disobedient and then punished.

Parents pass on their experiences, knowledge, conditioning, and culture—often dead, second-hand, outdated information—expecting us to preserve these traditions and ancient beliefs. We dutifully record every bit of this knowledge in our brains and develop our identities based on it. In this process, the joy and happiness we innately experienced as infants eventually gives way to anger, jealousy, and self-centeredness. As we age, we give up and blindly accept whatever knowledge our authority figures have taught us. When this doesn't work, and we cannot cope with life's innumerable problems, we begin to struggle.

My life today is not the same as it was when I was a young child. Things that were once beautiful no longer seem that way. Have I already imprinted in my brain pictures of the world's wonders—the sky and its innumerable stars, the majestic mountains, valleys, and the vast oceans—so I don't need to look at them again to be reminded of their beauty? When I occasionally observe and enjoy the beauty around me, I feel immensely happy, but real life quickly beckons me back to the 'battle'. Taking time off soon becomes monotonous, and I am eager to get back to work after a few days. Why does the beauty around me become a thing of joy for only short periods? Have I become so used to the mechanical routine of day-to-day life that I am unable to venture away from it for long? How did I get to be this way?

Growing up, I relied on parents and teachers to tell me what to do, how to behave and observe, follow, and imitate the so-called successful people around me. Trusting that they knew what was best, I always obeyed. I became convinced I was incapable of making any meaningful decisions for myself. I adopted this 'roadmap' for my life, never for a moment questioning it or realising that I had merely borrowed it from others. As I grew older, I tried to conform to this borrowed roadmap, even though it clearly didn't help me meet life's challenges. My great achievements in life became part of the extra 'baggage' I carried in a futile attempt to find happiness. Along with the tangible baggage like my bank balance, house, furniture, paintings, and education, I also carried fear, sorrow, unhappiness, jealousy, envy, frustration, and anger. My attempts to escape and find happiness, joy and a peaceful state of mind were always unsuccessful.

From an early age, I was taught that armed with the right education, I could accomplish just about anything in life. Knowledge reigned supreme, according to my parents and teachers. It was the perfect tool with which to manoeuvre through the treacherous journey of life, and the more knowledge, the better. Life was a battlefield, and if I didn't possess the right intellectual tools, I would lose the war to smarter people who could outwit me. Around every corner, something or somebody would be lurking, waiting to defeat me; therefore, I would need to be cautious of every step I took, always alert and armed with sufficient knowledge to defend myself.

To avoid being left behind, I would need to keep up with those around me who accumulated vast amounts of knowledge. To succeed in life and be respected, I had to have a strong educational foundation, and the fastest way to get this was to attend university and obtain a degree.

After earning a university degree and arming myself with a vast amount of knowledge, I met life's challenges with some degree of confidence. But despite all the knowledge and experience I had gained, I realised that most people were still uninterested in my beliefs or opinions. Over time, I discovered the reasons for this—all our opinions and beliefs are based on previous knowledge and experiences stored in our brain in the form of memories. For example, we like or dislike something to the extent of our prior experience. Our ego's role is to staunchly protect and defend these beliefs and opinions without question. When someone offers an opinion that may or may not conform to ours, we only pretend to listen to their views. At the same time, our brain continually searches the vast database in its memory bank for references and data to support our own convictions.

Eventually and thankfully, I concluded that my roadmap of previous knowledge would never lead me down the path to happiness; in fact, it would only hold me back. My choice was simple, but not easy. Would I continue carrying the baggage and lead the same old life of conflict, frustration, anxiety, emptiness, and confusion, or let go of all this baggage so I could live a life of everlasting joy? I had always been told that sorrow, anger, and pain were part of life, and I had become so attached to my baggage. I didn't think I could live without it. How could I possibly dispose of the baggage I had so painstakingly collected and carried all my life? Who would I be without my baggage? Would people respect me without it? Would they even recognise me? Would I be lonely?

How often do we stop to ask these questions? We don't even realise that it is possible to change the course of our lives. Why are we so scared to try something new? Do we think we are destined to lead the mechanical life we inherited from our parents and grandparents?

We express and mimic the conditioned behaviours of those

we watch. As a child, I inadvertently learned and observed everything around me—from my parents, teachers, and friends. Children first learn about the world through their parents. They become conditioned to think and act the same way their parents do from infancy. This is the same conditioning that the parents learned from their parents. Life becomes this endless stream of passing down conditioning to each new generation. As children, we don't question what we acquire from our parents, teachers, and friends. We simply accept it and continue to act and think as they did. It is as if we are downloading a corrupted software onto new hardware. The hardware being our uncorrupted young minds as children, and the corrupted software our parents preconditioned knowledge. Over time, because of the continual download of corrupted information, our hardware begins to lose efficiency and deteriorate.

We grow up, get married, start a family, and strive for success and power, only to experience jealousy, envy, fear, frustration, and unhappiness. When we do experience happiness and love, it is short-lived, providing only brief moments of respite. We wonder why we don't feel whole and hope that something or someone will 'complete' us in the future. Every moment of our lives, we struggle to find ourselves. We seek our friends, teachers, and society to answer our problems and become dependent upon them to fix our troubles. We have been programmed to ignore our own brains and instead listen to people who supposedly have immense knowledge and education.

Not knowing how to think for ourselves traps us in a prison

that feels familiar; we feel at home there. We decorate the walls with our achievements—degrees, accolades, status symbols—to make ourselves believe we are happy. But this happiness is temporary and unfulfilling at best. We feel a need to protect ourselves from others, which makes us feel separate and alone. We get caught in the grip of desire. We strive to achieve things in life and then become attached to those achievements—power, status, material possessions. The 'thought' of losing what we have achieved causes us great anxiety. We are unhappy and occasionally feel the urge to escape the prison, only to quickly slip back into its familiar confines.

What if the answer to our struggle is inside us? And our outdated thoughts and beliefs are the real cause of our conflict? We rarely stop to question the validity of the second-hand knowledge stored within our brains. Is it possible that this knowledge we work so hard to acquire and protect is hindering us? Why have our attempts to find an alternate way of living been so unsuccessful? Why have we been unable to make this shift? Are we waiting for someone to show us the way? Is it even possible to create such a life for ourselves? There must be more in life than this ...

Thirteen

Crossing Paths Deep Within

*Experiencing unconditional love for everyone
and everything, including all the miracles that
make us who we are.*

I t seems to me that on the biopsy table, all my arrogance, ego, anger, hatred and jealousy dissolved. For the first time in my life, I came face to face with my own conditioned 'self'. Did the acceptance of my own mortality help me dissolve the conditioned baggage that I had been carrying for so long? It was as if the realisation of my own conditioned 'self' helped free me from its clutches. Being so close to death made me realise how trivial everything was within our single-minded society. The only thing that mattered to me was living another day. I felt like a child again—free. As though I could run wild across the paddy field, whooping in joy. I had been trapped in the casket of adulthood and lost my childhood innocence. This is one of the greatest mistakes we make, neglecting and hiding our innate curiosity and creativity. As we mature, we give up the youthful energy from our childhood, resulting in mediocre and unfulfilling lives.

All my life, I had lived selfishly, striving to make a name for myself. Following this painful ordeal, I realised that I had never stopped to consider other people's sensitivities. I think I got sick for a reason. The intense suffering came with a message. It made me realise how wrong I was about the world and about life. I had always believed that my purpose was to succeed and make lots of money so that I could live luxuriously. Now I realise that our manifestation as humans on this planet has a greater purpose.

I used to be the type of person who didn't even consider that other people have feelings, let alone try and empathise with what they might be going through. After my ordeal, I started noticing the strain, pain, and emotion on people's faces. I saw how tired people were. I saw fear and anxiety etched into my colleagues' faces—anxiety about work, fear for their jobs. I witnessed the random acts of kindness that people shared, even with strangers. How a simple smile had the power to change someone's day.

When I look back, many individuals came to help and support me during those difficult times of suffering. The doctors and nurses, my in-laws, my parents, my brother and sister, locals in Perth, and most of all, my wife, who nursed me back to life and gave me a second chance at life. She gave me strength and courage when I couldn't see the light within the darkness of my illness. She cared for me with unconditional love and showed me how to overcome life's greatest challenges with humility. When I used to experience severe back and chest pain at night, she gently placed her hand over my chest as if attempting to take the pain away. It was comforting, and I often felt a divine energy pass through me from her. I am eternally grateful to all those who came into my life and helped me embrace my rebirth.

For the first time in a long time, my life was about noticing others and witnessing the true meaning of unconditional love. Many of us express love to those who are close to us. However, unconditional love is a true phenomenon. The love you feel for all living creatures is the same. It is unlimited and extends beyond life and death. There is no attachment, nor any expectation of getting anything in return, just pure compassion, which has the power to vanquish any force. Although our world may be filled with suffering, fear, war, and violence, if we can appreciate love and extend unconditional love to those around us, we can preserve humanity.

I have encountered many challenges throughout life, and though tedious, I have tried to embrace and learn from each circumstance. I see them as miracles, helping me connect with inspiring and compassionate individuals, guiding me to be a more empathetic being.

One miraculous interaction that continues to influence me is my encounter with a man named Tom. It was truly a miracle of interaction, almost like an angel who came to guide me. It occurred a few years after my medical incident when I was still striving to find out my purpose in life.

It was a beautiful morning with rays of golden sun streaming across the wide blue expanse of space above us. The street was empty, apart from an elderly man rolling a shopping trolley just a couple of metres ahead. I paced along the sidewalk, my head churning with thoughts. Although I was beginning to become more aware of the conditioned baggage that prevented me from fully flowering in life, I still lived with the confusion of discovering my purpose in life. The mediocre cycle of life, where we are born and live our life merely struggling to exist, seemed completely futile. We spend years at school being inundated with information and rote learning to pass exams. We manage to get a job, where we must work to earn money to survive, buy a house, get married and have children. We invest all our time and money into educating and raising our children and find happiness through their successes and achievements before finally reaching our inevitable demise. During those years, we may have some moments of happiness, excitement, love, as well as anger, anxiety, loss, jealousy, but I still wondered: *Did we truly live our lives?* There had to be more to life than this vain existence.

So, despite having come this far, I still felt incomplete. I knew that I couldn't complain, as I was in a comfortable situation. I had climbed the corporate ladder and become the CEO of a Biotech company based in Melbourne. Having done the same thing for several years, I had begun to get this yearning to try something new. I didn't want to be in the same position for the rest of my working life. It was quite ironic because, for most of my life, this had been my dream; however, now I didn't want that life. The intense suffering that I encountered dramatically changed my perspective on life. *Now what? Why did I still feel so incomplete?*

I felt completely lost, with no idea what my future could hold. I knew that I couldn't continue down the same path. I didn't know who to ask for help. Even though I had so many people in my life, I felt alone. No one would understand what I was going through. It was like a midlife crisis. Everyone was proud of how successful my life was turning out. I had achieved everything that I had aspired to, yet I didn't want it anymore. It was the life teenage Santosh had dreamed of. The life he wanted so he could prove to everyone that he was, in fact, 'worth it'.

Suddenly, I came to a standstill. The elderly man, a few steps ahead of me, abruptly stopped. His body trembled. As he began to lose balance and fall, he lost his grip on his trolley, and it rolled forwards, colliding with a lamppost, spilling its contents across the pathway. I ran, reaching him in a long stride. I dropped onto my knees, supporting his neck and head. His eyes were closed and his breath was shallow. I reached into my pocket and pulled out my phone, immediately dialling for the ambulance. The ambulance arrived within minutes, while I sat next to the man, supporting him. The paramedics checked his vitals while loading him into the vehicle. As they were tending to him, I ran to pick up the trolley contents and placed everything inside before following the paramedics into the ambulance. They immediately bombarded me with questions, writing down all the details. I recounted the fact that he was just walking in front of me when he collapsed.

I sat in the ambulance in a daze as we flew through streets and past cars, the sirens sounding loudly. Within no time, we had reached the hospital. The paramedics wheeled the stretcher out and took the man to the emergency department. They took him so quickly that I had no chance to find out where they were going. I was just about to rush after them when the paramedics said that he would be fine, and I was good to go. They thanked me for my kind gesture and then departed, as they were called for another duty. I knew that there was little I could do to help now, as the medical experts would take care of him. So, I wheeled the trolley and walked home.

That afternoon, I decided to go back to the hospital to check on him, as I still had his trolley. I went to the front desk and inquired about him. They asked me to wait, so I found a seat, resting the trolley beside me. I must have been exhausted as I fell asleep against the wall and woke up to someone gently tapping my shoulder. I opened my eyes and saw a doctor standing in front of me. He smiled as I woke, momentarily confused. Then it dawned on me that I came to check on the man.

'Is he a relative?' the doctor asked. I immediately recounted the incidents of that morning. The doctor nodded and ushered me through the hospital corridors to a room. 'He is alright now. He just suffered from low blood pressure. He just needs some rest. Although he is okay to go home sometime today. I'll come in and check on him in a few moments.'

When we reached the room, I thanked the doctor, shaking his hand before gently knocking on the door, waiting for a reply. I entered once I heard a strong voice reply. Light flooded the small room. The elderly man was sitting up in his bed, staring out the window. He looked like he was in his late seventies, with wrinkles crinkling his brown weathered skin from a life spent in the sun. He had a strong bone structure beneath the wrinkles, giving a glimpse of the confident and strong man he must have been in his youth. He had receding white hair—a stark contrast to his tan skin. He looked older in the hospital bed surrounded by white sheets and walls. But his grey expressive eyes revealed a happy, younger man. I was glad to see that he looked healthy and awake. I wheeled the trolley in and parked it at the end of his bed. 'Hi, I'm Santosh. I saw you collapse on the street; I was right behind you.' He nodded and smiled in appreciation. 'How are you feeling?'

He replied in a calm, yet confident voice, 'Much better, thanks to you. I'm not sure what happened today. I was walking down the street with my shopping, and the next thing I remember is being in the hospital.' He smiled, and I felt at ease. He was evidently the type of person who radiated good energy.

When the doctor walked in, he greeted the old man jovially and the old man smiled at him. As the doctor checked his vitals, he confirmed that it was okay for him to go home. The man thanked the doctor, giving him a heartfelt handshake and hug. As the doctor left, I asked the man whether I could drop him home. 'That would be great,' he replied.

Once his trolley was stowed safely in the boot, we drove in comfortable silence, just enjoying the beautiful day. I asked for his address, which was close to where we had been walking that morning.

'Whereabouts do you live, young man?'

I smiled. 'Not far from you, actually. Just down the road at Zala Court.' He nodded in recognition.

Suddenly, I realised that I didn't know his name, so I asked, and he laughed. 'I'm sorry, Santosh, I think I forgot to introduce myself, although we didn't really get the opportunity with me collapsing and that ...' He smiled warmly. 'My name is Tom Samson.' He explained that he was retired and lived alone in a retirement village. I knew the place; it was close to where I lived. A beautiful little community, with perfect small homes that all looked similar—homely cottages with manicured gardens. The community was nicely secluded from the rush and noise of the main road, near a quiet tree-lined lake.

I parked in front of his house, which was immaculate with velvety green grass and small flowers near the front window. Tom got out, fumbling with the keys in his pocket, while I went to get his trolley and wheeled it inside. Tom's house wasn't grand, but it was obvious that he cared for it. I also noticed the many potted plants throughout the house. As I followed Tom into his spotless kitchen, wheeling the trolley behind me, I was greeted by old Victorian wooden shelves and white marble benches overlooking a beautifully tended back garden. Bursts of colour erupted from the many flowers, and the drooping branches of his hanging willow tree swayed in the summer breeze. Tom's home was a personification of his charisma. It exuded charm, tranquillity and silence. 'Beautiful house,' I told him.

He looked over and smiled. 'I love it too. We take care of each other. I take care of her by maintaining her and keeping her clean, and she provides me with shelter and a home.' I smiled to myself. He was such a unique character. 'Would you like some tea?' he asked.

'That would be nice,' I replied. As Tom put the kettle on, I helped him unload his shopping trolley. We worked together quietly while I brought out all the groceries from the bag. Tom placed them in their rightful places. When we were done, Tom poured the water into the tea and added some milk and sugar. He handed me my cup and led me towards his living room. I sat on the lovely blue couch, sinking into its cushions as Tom sat down on a peach armchair that seemed old yet loved. We sat there, enjoying the beautiful aura of the room, listening to the birds chirping outside and the soft rolls of the wind. I put my cup down on the coaster in front of me and turned towards Tom. I was curious. He seemed like he knew so much. I wanted to know more about him.

He smiled at me, encouraging me to speak. He seemed to know that I wanted to ask him something. Over the cup of tea, I learned that he had lived on his own in this home for the past six years since his beloved wife Julie had passed away. He had one son who lived in Germany with his young family. It had been about three years since he last saw his son, because it was hard for them to come down.

It must be a lonely life, I thought. Despite being alone, Tom lived his life happily and fully. He loved gardening, so he spent hours tending his garden and the community garden down the road. He explained how all his plants were like his friends, sharing their unconditional love with him through their magnificent beauty. He volunteered with the local library, reading books to children. He also spent time on Sundays playing golf with his old friends. He seemed content. His life was such a different way of living compared to mine. He had no commitments, no expectations, no stresses, no family, no attachment. He seemed genuinely free. 'So, Santosh, I want to know about you. You're a young man with so much more ahead of you. Tell me more about yourself. What were you doing outside this morning?' he asked with genuine curiosity. I shook my head bemusedly, unsure where to begin.

The sun had begun to set, and the day had begun to cool down. I didn't realise how much time passed as I recounted everything that I had experienced: my ambition for success, my medical ordeal, my transformation, my present confusion. As I let everything out, Tom sat silently, listening with rapt attention. He never interrupted with an opinion or judgement, nor did he provide feedback throughout my story. He just sat and let me empty out everything.

For the first time, I felt my burdens dissolving. I expressed how incomplete I felt now and how I had no idea what to do next. Tom merely raised his eyebrows, contemplating something. When I finally finished my recount, Tom sank back comfortably in his chair and looked out the window, his forehead creased in thought. He turned towards me with a serious expression and asked, 'What is it that you really want from life? What do you want to do with the rest of your life? What is your passion?'

I sat staring at him, completely confounded. *My passion?* At that moment, Tom's landline rang. Excusing himself, he got up from his chair to take the call. Realising that it was now dusk, I knew that it was time to go. I think I may have extended my invitation and burdened him with all my problems, the poor man. I picked up the empty teacups and went to the sink to rinse them. I decided that it was probably time to leave, but I didn't want to interrupt him during his conversation, so I tapped on his shoulder and motioned I was leaving. I mouthed thank you and was about to turn around to leave. Tom motioned for me to wait, so I stayed where I was while he paused his conversation with the person on the other line. He placed his phone down and came towards me for a hug. He patted me on the back in a fatherly way and told me that he was grateful for what I did today and for our time together. I thanked him for his kindness and patience and went to my car. I waved goodbye to the small figure of Tom as I drove further and further from his picturesque home.

During the drive home, my mind kept mulling over the comment that Tom made. *What is my passion? What is the purpose of my life?* I never even considered these questions. I never once thought I was born for a reason, that I was given my second chance at life for a reason. Like most people, I just focused on getting through life as successfully as possible. I lived most of my life trying to prove myself and others against the label 'good for nothing'. I had strived to achieve monetary and corporate success; however, nothing had ever made me genuinely happy. Now I understood that I hadn't achieved any of those things for myself. It was merely to prove to those around me. This was not what I was meant to do. There had to be more. My brain contemplated all the possibilities for a passion, but nothing came to mind. That night I fell asleep early, exhausted by the day and my extended introspection.

*   *   *

For the next few days, I was busy at work. I travelled interstate for meetings and conferences. Tired and worn out by the travel and demanding work, I didn't have the time to contemplate my passion. It was only on the weekend, after a whole week away, that I woke up in the morning with the eagerness and time to consider what to do next. But first I wanted to go to meet Tom. I hadn't been able to check in on him and see how he was after the last time. I also enjoyed being in his calming presence, as it helped me feel more centred. As I drove towards Tom's home, I realised that it was such a beautiful day, with clear skies and the golden rays reflecting against the still waters of the calm blue lake. It was so quiet and peaceful that even the trees seemed to be perfectly still without a single rustle or brush of a leaf. I parked my car in front of Tom's little cottage, collecting his mail. He had quite a lot of mail on that day, so I carried it in with me. I knocked on his door gently and waited a few minutes. No one came, nor was there any noise on the other side. I knocked again, this time stronger. Nothing. I looked down at my watch— quarter-past ten. Maybe he had gone somewhere. I decided to drop in at the visitor's centre and enquire where he might be while also giving them his mail.

When I reached the visitor's desk, a kind elderly lady greeted me. I enquired about Tom, letting her know that I was a friend. Her expression changed as I mentioned his name, from one of open kindness to melancholy. Her eyes met mine, and I saw her sadness and regret. My heart sank, and my breathing grew shallow as she swallowed before slowly saying that Tom had passed away a few days before.

Tears welled in my eyes and my throat constricted. I had known that it was bad news, but my brain was taking its time to comprehend the meaning of her words. Tom was gone. Gone forever. I would never see him again. She looked at me in sympathy and explained that he died peacefully. He had apparently been struggling with type 2 diabetes for a while, and one night his body just seemed to give way. I thanked her and walked out. I didn't know where I was going, but my feet just dragged me along. I walked to a park bench and collapsed onto it. Head between my hands and elbows on my knees, I sat there staring at the concrete path under my feet. I had only just begun to get to know him, and he was taken away so soon.

After a few moments, I noticed a golden leaf drifting from the sky before landing at my feet. I looked up to see the broad branches of an autumnal beech tree. The gold and red-hued leaves were gently reaching for the welcoming earth, showing off their stunning colours one final time. Before touching the ground, they danced around, twirling in the wind, perhaps to let the whole world know they had realised their true purpose on earth, and it was time to say goodbye—a real example of selfless existence, indeed! I thought to myself: *Like these leaves, have I found the real purpose of my existence on Earth?*

I needed to find my inner calling, my true passion. I began to question what that might be. To find the answer, I needed to go deep within. I decided to pursue this question even more now that I had been given a chance to continue living.

Could it be that Tom was sent to me for a reason? To help me solve the puzzle that I was struggling with? He guided me and then vanished forever—my guardian angel. It was beyond what I could comprehend. May his soul rest in peace. He deserved it. Feeling tired and heavy with loss and confusion, I slowly walked back to my car and drove back home with an abundance of sadness and gratitude in my heart.

*   *   *

Over the next few weeks, life continued to roll on. My discovery of the truth was far from over, although it was progressing. I was working on two puzzles now. Self-discovery, figuring out the root cause of all my conditioning, in other words—*Who am I?* And searching for the purpose of my manifestation—*Why was I given a second opportunity at life?* I felt that these two questions were somehow connected. My self-discovery of the truth may help provide light in discovering the purpose of my life. I didn't know for sure, but I was determined to find out. I wanted to utilise the energy that Tom passed on to me during his last few days. He was the epitome of a different way of life—a life of contentment and meaning.

Fourteen

Discovery of Space

Stopping the pendulum by observing
the spaces in-between.

One afternoon, I decided to experiment with my mind. I drove down the quiet afternoon roads towards the peaceful and secluded lake near Tom's house. I drove into the retirement home, feeling a sense of nostalgia. I drove past Tom's house, quickly glancing away from the 'For Sale' sign and turned towards the sparkling blue of the reflecting waters. Parking my car, I found a park bench and took a seat facing the water. I sat there feeling the warmth of the sun on my back. *Okay, so let's try this out*, I thought. I closed my eyes and tuned into the noise within my head. As I realised earlier, the brain is constantly engaged in the thinking process. Most of the time, we are unaware of the incessant noise going on in our minds.

As I observed my mind, I realised that although the movement of my thoughts seem swift and ongoing, there were gaps. A gap in which a thought comes to an end and a new thought hasn't yet appeared. As I sat there on the garden chair, multiple thoughts inundated my head. In my determined haste to begin my exploration, I had neglected my morning coffee, and now my body was craving its morning kick. My mind dug up images of my favourite café—the crafted wooden chairs, glassed wooden tabletops, rustic brick walls, and strong aroma of roasting coffee. Within another microsecond, my mind flashed to the vegetable focaccia that was such a great accompaniment to my frothy coffee. Instantly, my mind flashed to the meeting that I had with my friend last week at the café, and how I was meant to get back to him regarding a date and time for our next meeting. Immediately, my hand moved towards my pocket to retrieve my phone so that I could respond. Just in time, I stopped myself.

In between each thought—the coffee, the focaccia, the meeting—there was a minuscule gap. And in that moment when I realised that I was responding to the thought about finalising the date with my friend, there was another gap. A gap in which I realised I had been thinking. This space or gap isn't related to the thought process. We don't usually notice this space. But if you observe carefully, you will become aware that it is full of silence. A brief space in which there is no thought—just space and silence. This space may be the missing piece in our lives! Not knowing that this space exists may be the root cause of all our problems. Yet how does this space free us from the mind?

Awareness of this space—fully experiencing this space—can liberate us from our past conditioning. It can liberate us from our conditioned baggage. Ultimately, freeing us from our memories and learned emotions which have ruled our lives thus far. By recognising and dwelling in this space, thought activity itself comes to an end. The pendulum stops right in the middle. At this moment, we experience a momentary feeling of peace and silence.

I realised that this space of peace had been missing from my life, and to experience a more fulfilling life, I needed to expand this space of awareness. I needed to expand the space between my thoughts and reduce my thought activity.

I leaned forwards, opening my eyes to the golden brightness of the lake. I groaned in frustration. *Well, how do I do that? How do I expand this so-called 'space' in my life?* Despite having read so many books on spirituality, achieving enlightenment, and meditation, they never once explained how to achieve that space of peace. I leaned back, raising my head towards the sky. I closed my eyes against the afternoon brightness and pinched the bridge of my nose. *This whole questioning process and discovery of the truth keeps getting harder and harder, while the truth gets deeper and deeper. Why is it so hard to figure it out? Is it because I am using my mind to figure it out? Perhaps? It It all seems so intricately complex. Bewildering.*

Despite the confusion, I could feel that the answer was close, prompting me to figure it out. *How to achieve that space of peace? How can I bring it into my life?* Many sources explained that meditating for at least twenty minutes every morning would help bring peace. Yes, during those twenty minutes, it always helped me feel so calm and still. What about after those twenty minutes? The beginning of my day would be relaxing and peaceful, but by the time I was halfway through, I would once again be tired, restless, and anxious from the business and rush of the day. There had to be more. *How can I bring presence or remain conscious (aware) every moment of my life without being dragged into the madness (anger, fear, anxiety, stress) of day-to-day life?*

*   *   *

During my meditation every morning, I endeavoured to observe my mind. I watched it like a guard on alert for when a stray thought popped up. I was simply observing the thoughts as they appeared, accepting them instead of forcing them away. Through time and effort, I realised that inhibiting my thoughts and forcing myself not to think was like fighting a never-ending battle. I was just going to war with myself.

I learned this the hard way. Initially, I would sit down in my comfortable lounge chair, close my eyes, and force myself to concentrate. I would strain my focus towards this dark dot behind my eyelids and concentrate on keeping thoughts out. However, most of the time, a deceptive thought would squeeze through, capturing my attention completely. I would drift along with the thought, resulting in a cascade of thoughts inundating me. Then I would realise that I had lost my focus. Frustrated and discouraged, I would again force myself to concentrate. But all I could hear in my mind was the constant scathing voice telling me that I couldn't do it. I kept trying to achieve a sense of peace, so I was searching for something extraordinary. I imagined that some form of energy would fill my body, and I would glow with a golden halo. Little did I realise that this yearning for achieving a specific state of mind was, in fact, mind conceived. The whole process was futile because I was trying to fight the mind with the mind. To truly discover the truth, I had to go beyond the mind. And the only way to go beyond anything is to first accept it. I had to accept or become aware of my persistent mind. I had to accept my thoughts, not resist them.

I also remembered something that I had once heard in a meditation video online. 'Imagine yourself to be the vast sky, and each individual thought to be a passing cloud. When a cloud comes, merely let it pass. Don't try to push it away because another will just appear. Just observe the passing cloud and acknowledge its existence. It will pass on its own.'

So, that's what I began doing. New thoughts constantly came into my mind. However, instead of struggling, I would merely watch them drifting in and out. Because of this, they no longer affected me. I used to constantly feel the need to react to my thoughts, to do something with them. When a thought that made me angry surfaced, I would react and become angry. Likewise, when a satisfying thought came to me, I would feel happy. I was at the complete mercy of these transient and intangible thoughts.

Now, when a thought comes into my head, I do not identify with it. I do not give it the power, energy, or attention. I simply observe the thought with full awareness, becoming aware of the mental activity. Let it come and let it pass, but don't identify with it. Just as the clouds come and go in the vast sky, thoughts, feelings, and sensations will simply arise and pass away. The clouds don't and cannot overwhelm the vast sky, and neither should our thoughts, feelings, and sensations.

Although I had thought that I had gained freedom following my medical diagnosis, there's a feeling of immense relief when you have complete control of yourself. I know that many people spend years trying to figure out who they are. However, to truly feel comfortable in our own bodies, we need to have the autonomy to control our own emotions, thoughts, and behaviours. Until this moment, I had felt as though I was trapped within my own body, watching things happen through my eyes. However, my actions and words were never truly my own. I was never really myself. I had become lost somewhere throughout my upbringing, and now I had finally found a home.

With the awareness of my thoughts,
I was able to have power over my mind,
and therefore it no longer controlled me.

*   *   *

Initially, I used my morning meditation to observe my mind for just ten minutes. I gradually increased this time to thirty. I would sit on a comfortable chair, relaxing my spine and the muscles in my neck and back. Then, I observed the activity within my head. Merely watching it and noticing it: *Look, another thought. There goes another one. Yep, another one.* I wouldn't judge my thoughts, because as soon as we begin judging or evaluating, the mind is again at play, as only the mind judges.

Over time, with practice, we can observe the thoughts arising and subsiding. If our mind is judging, we need to observe that judgement. Become aware of it, rather than suppress it. We need to notice any emotions that arise within us. We may feel restless, bored. However, we need to observe that feeling. Accept that our mind is bored. When we are mindful and observe these thoughts and emotions attentively, we will not allow these emotions or thoughts to overpower us or act through us. We need to strive to be a mindful observer moment to moment, every moment.

It's like breaking a habit. Our old habit was to constantly be unaware of our own minds, allowing them to take control of us. Through meditation, I challenged this old habit, rewiring my brain to become more aware. It's pure biology. Habits are formed and made by certain actions and thoughts. These actions and thoughts are controlled by the neural connections within our brains. These neural connections are like pathways in our brain. As we continue to strengthen a pathway by reinforcing a particular behaviour, the pathway becomes more established. Almost cemented. I visualise this by imagining a pathway in a forest. The path is covered in tiny pebbles and worn by multiple travellers, giving you a clear way forwards, much like our present conditioning. It is a solid path that has been reinforced for years. However, over time, the path is no longer used.

Years later, the path that was once lined with pebbles has been obscured by overgrown grass, flowers, and moss. It's no longer visible and no one uses it anymore. In the same way, by reconditioning our neurons, we can essentially rewire the connections in our brain that make us unconscious and struggling from incessant thinking. Instead, we can create a new pathway that enables us to bring constant awareness into our lives by reminding ourselves to be 'aware'. As we continue to bring awareness into our lives, this neural connection gets stronger, and our time of awareness increases. Over time and with practice, the neural pathway becomes so strong and reinforced that being constantly aware becomes second nature.

* * *

Each day, I could feel the space between each thought increasing, giving me more peace and clarity. Over time, this space wasn't limited to the thirty minutes in the morning. I began to use it throughout my day. I controlled the flow of thoughts by simultaneously observing what was occurring within me. All I had to do was to remember to be constantly aware. While I was doing anything, I just had to be completely conscious of what was going on in my mind by asking the simple question: *What am I thinking? Am I conscious at this moment?* Slowly, the brain becomes conditioned to this new way of thinking, of living.

The moment we ask, 'What am I thinking?', we become mindful of our thought activity, and there are no more thoughts. We have come back to the present—welcoming space and silence into our lives. The space is always there, just obscured by thoughts.

Ask yourself: 'What am I thinking now?' This question brings you back from whatever you are thinking, either about the past or the future, back to the present moment. How often can you remind yourself to ask this question in a day? Initially, it may be just a few times. With practice, you may be able to do so several times, and then with even more practice, you do not need to ask this question at all, as it becomes second nature. You are always in the present moment. Because you are mindful, you will catch yourself from moving back into the thought-dominated world of the past and future.

If you feel angry, upset, stressed, lonely, anxious, or fearful, know that you have moved away from being in the present moment. Bring yourself back quickly to the primordial state of being in the present. In the present, everything is as good as it can be. There are no worries of the past or anxiety of the future. Get rooted in this moment. Be mindful. Remember, thoughts give rise to the conditioned behaviours that you experience.

Awareness of fear dissolves fear. Awareness of anger dissolves anger. Awareness of any emotion dissolves that emotion. The difference is, previously, you were unaware of the emotions overpowering you. You are now fully aware of these emotions, and therefore, they don't overpower you and react through you anymore. Effectively, with your newfound awareness, a new world emerges, a world of peace and freedom. A world that has always been there for you but has been obscured by the mechanisms of the mind.

Fifteen

Space Within and Without

There is an abundance of space in which to find peace.

O nce I got used to meditating with my eyes closed and ensuring that my mind was rooted in the present moment, I attempted it with my eyes open. The main challenge with this is that there are many things around you, so your mind begins to judge these objects, taking you away from the present moment. Therefore, it takes more energy to be mindful. Our mind can be very cunning, and even the mere distraction of furniture or people can spur it to overwhelm you with thoughts. Our material lives are consumed by thing after thing and thought after thought, and it is immensely difficult to be in the present when the external world proves to be so distracting.

Over time I noticed one thing that was constant in our changing and unpredictable external world—the eternal space.

As I noticed the space in my mind, I finally began noticing the abundance of space around me. *But how often do we notice this space?* Especially, as it is obscured by the 'things' around us.

It all starts when we are young, when we are encouraged to be fascinated by toys and objects. Our parents point out objects, describing them with a word, and over time we start to feel a sense of possession over these toys. As we grow, we want more and more toys. We accumulate more toys, bigger, more expensive toys—the newest iPhone; the latest, fastest car; a house or houses; branded clothing, and shoes. Due to this accumulation of things, and the development of an identity defined by things, we completely lose sight of the space around us.

When I used to go for evening walks at the lake near my house, I would look up at the vastness of the aquamarine sky. I would notice all the things that happen within it. The sun dipping below the skyline, bruising the sky in hues of gold, pinks, and violets. The dark silhouettes of migratory birds flying north to warmer weather. Sometimes the odd cruising plane would make an entrance, shining against the rays of the sun. Then as the sun disappears, the moon comes up shining in all its glory. And behind the nail-shaped crescent, the dark, black expanse of the sky seems so overwhelming and eternal. Coming back to earth, trees and flowers need space between them to grow and flourish. Everything in the cosmos is arranged neatly in order, with 'perfect space' between them.

All different life forms—humans, plants and micro-organisms—originate, thrive, and perish within the external space. The sun ascends from and retires into this space. Wind arises and passes away; the rain also casts its spell and vanishes into space. Birth and death constantly happen in this space.

However, even though the space is ever-present, eternal, and always watching, we are so often negligent of it.

I realised that to gain peace in my life, I needed to become reacquainted with space—internally and externally. I needed to become familiar with its quietness, peace and energy. In my attempt to notice the Divine space, I began to look past things. I would observe the space between all the things in my life. When I went for my morning walks, I marvelled at the space surrounding the lake, above the rippling water of the lake. And within that space, I saw rays of light refracting across the surface of the lake, insects darting around, and birds tittering on some of the broad overhanging branches. I noticed all these things happening within that space. I noticed the newness and a newfound beauty all around me, beyond what words can describe.

Previously, I only noticed the trees and nature, always neglecting the most important part of nature—the space, and its associated tranquillity. I realised that once I embraced and observed the space, my mind was no longer as inundated. My thought activity ceased. Perhaps the main reason for this is that when we observe the space, there are no 'things' in the way. We are observing something that has no form. Space is intangible, and therefore unable to be judged or remembered as a memory. It is eternal, yet it is always new. Our mind is silenced, and we are finally able to connect with this external space, paving the way for true joy and tranquillity.

When we notice the space—the space of silence—we experience a period of no thoughts. The space within us recognises the space without. At that moment we no longer identify with our body and the baggage associated with it. We are not attached to our past conditioning, so there is no longer any fear or anxiety. We are freed from our self-induced prison. We realise that we are the space. The body has a finite life; however, we are not that body. We are the space in which the body and other forms come and go. All energy in the universe is the same, just manifested in different forms. Hence, we are all forms of manifested consciousness, awareness, mindfulness, nothingness, higher energy, or simply put, the eternal space. This is not a spiritual or philosophical fantasy. We simply know this when the mind activity comes to a halt—when we are in the present. This can neither be described in words nor taught. *Can we ever describe the space? Can we describe that which is formless?* When you describe that state of presence to someone, you are simply narrating a past experience stored in your memory. This means you have moved away from being in the present.

I began using this space to help stay in the present, and soon everywhere I looked, I could see space. While driving to work, inside the car, outside on the road, between my car and the one in front of me, above me. At night, when lying in bed and several thoughts came into my head, I turned my attention to the vast space around me—the space above, the space to the sides, and the space beneath the curve of my spine. In this way, the incessant thought activity dissolved, and I found myself back in the present moment.

I even used this technique with people, noticing the space that surrounded people rather than the person themselves. When I looked at the person, my mind immediately formed judgements. Instead, I noticed the space around them, surrounding them, the space between the person and me. As I did this, I realised that I was no longer looking through my conditioned mind's filters. There was no barrier between me and the other being—just a sense of oneness with everyone and everything. Unlike 'things' found in this space, the emptiness cannot be judged. There is no movement of thought when we observe this space—no mental projections.

This way of living may be difficult to comprehend. It is not within reach of the 'normal conditioned' mind. However, the normal mind's workings are precisely what prevent us from recognising that we are one with space. The mind separates us from recognising space and from each other. So, we need to learn how to slow down the incessant movement of our mind pendulum and allow it to come to a standstill—allowing us to embrace eternal space, bringing clarity and beauty in our lives. As soon as we tap into the space—life energy—we feel oneness. The knowing that we are no longer a separate entity. Rather, we are one with vast space. We are space.

Sixteen

You took my Breath away

Pointers to the now are everywhere.

One morning, as I sat in front of my home desktop scanning through emails, my mind flashed with various thoughts. Noticing the overwhelming noise in my mind, I leaned my head back against my chair and closed my eyes to let my mind come back to a standstill—inviting the calmness and clarity of space to enter.

After a few moments, I opened my eyes and took a few deep breaths of air while rolling my tense shoulders back, easing the tight muscles. As I took a deep breath to clear my mind, I once again became aware of the external space surrounding me. The cool air of the space surrounding me wafted up my nose, filling my lungs and becoming a part of my internal space. The slow rhythmic process seemed so easy to follow, and it scared me how I had so easily neglected to notice the subconscious process that was always occurring within me. We so often take our breath for granted. But when we notice our breath, when we become mindful of the natural and cyclic process, we discover that there is no room for thoughts. Instead, space opens within us. Space becomes available because we are resting solidly in the present, mindful of each refreshing breath. The moment this attention wavers, the moment we are unmindful of our slow breathing, we allow thoughts to enter, taking us back into the past or forwards into the future—we are no longer in the present moment.

I realised that being mindful of my own breathing worked as a way of bringing me back to a place of peace. Every time I inhaled, I felt myself taking air from vast space, and when I exhaled, I was breathing out into that vast Divine space—my breath being the connection between the external and internal space.

Sitting forwards in my chair, I considered how extraordinary this pointer was. It is always within us, the rhythm of life as steady as it is reliable. It is the easiest pointer or technique to use when we want an immediate source of space and peace. All we must do is bring our attention back to the subconscious act of inhaling and exhaling. Thereby bringing us back into the present moment.

I used my breath while working, walking, driving and before going to sleep. It's such a calming source of guidance, as nothing is more definite and present than the breath you are taking now.

*   *   *

The miraculous thing about using breathing as a pointer is that when we focus our attention on our breath, it also makes us more aware of our body. I noticed that when I recognised the passive process of my breathing, I immediately realised that my posture was tense, or I was subconsciously shaking my leg. As I observed, I noticed the stress in my back muscles and the creeping symptoms of a headache, as well as the emptiness of my stomach. From this, I recognised that by focusing on my body, I could bring my mind to the present moment. However, this pointer proved to be more powerful than just bringing my mind to the present. It was also therapeutic.

It's surprising how little attention we pay to our bodies. Often we only begin to become aware of how much we take our bodies for granted when we become diseased. However, when we listen and pay attention to the body, we begin to understand and respect it. Our bodies tell us so much about our health, but we blatantly ignore the signs and symptoms.

Some nights I found it difficult to go to sleep. My brain was restless, churning with thoughts, and my back ached from hours of bad posture. However, as I lay with my back against the mattress, I began to use this pointer to listen to, and relax, my body and mind.

First, I would focus on my feet, just noticing them, curling the toes, and easing the day's pressure. I began to appreciate how important feet are, how they have carried my weight tirelessly since the day I took those first unsteady steps as an infant. I would then allow my attention to travel up my calves, releasing the tension built up in them from the hour of driving on the stagnant freeway. Slowly moving my attention to the rest of my legs, I became aware of the weight of them sinking into the bed. Then I would move towards my back, noticing where I sank into the mattress and where the curve of my spine created a tiny space between the bed and feeling the soft fabric of my pyjamas on the surface of my skin.

I would then allow my awareness to drift across my back, relaxing each muscle, the tight cords of muscle around my spinal column, and those small tendons supporting the head. My awareness would drift along the length of my arms to my fingers and back up to my shoulders, noticing the dull ache in my right shoulder, easing the pain. I would allow myself to explore the tiny muscles and sensations of my face, exploring the tension in my jaw and the way my forehead felt permanently creased. By the time I had scanned and observed my entire body, I felt so relaxed. It was like a massage, relieving the stress from each cell in my own body.

Using the body scan, I was able to bring my awareness to the processes and sensations of my body, bringing my mind to the present moment. This may be because whatever is occurring in the body is occurring at that moment. Therefore, our mind is unable to wander. When certain thoughts drifted into my head, I would also try to become aware of its activity, just as I had practised, allowing myself to come back once again to the present moment.

Seventeen

Touch of Silence

Noticing the abundance of sounds
that drift over and through us.

One day, following a perfectly crazy morning with my family—answering the ridiculous yet curious questions posed by my teenage daughter and the subtle demands from my son for another new game for his Xbox—I was on my way to my office. Again, trapped in traffic, the cars were end-to-end, waiting for the train to pass at the railway crossing. I looked towards the car next to me on the right. The woman inside was staring at the crossings, drumming her fingers on the steering wheel. Frustrated by the wait, she slammed her hand against the steering wheel and slumped back into her seat. I smiled to myself, recognising the frustration.

These days I see how futile it is to feel frustrated by traffic. There is nothing we can do to get out of it once stuck in it. There's nothing we can do to speed up the railway crossing. So, what's the point in getting all worked up over something we can't control? I now knew how unnecessary stress was so detrimental to my health. I turned back to the road and opened my windows to let in some fresh air. Resting my arm on the windowsill, I heard the vibration of the track as the train rolled its way closer to us. The dull hum of the vibration became louder, and slowly I noticed that it changed to become a mellow drumming sound. The vibration grew louder and louder, becoming so loud that it overpowered all the other sounds around us. As rapidly as the deep sound arrived, it slowly disappeared into the distance as the train became a tiny speck on the unending railway line. Then, as the boom gates opened to allow us through, the low rumble of engines coming to life resounded through the air, followed by the deafening sounds of cars as they picked up speed. I shook myself out of my reverie, accelerating before the person behind me became impatient.

Sound is such an important stimulus in our lives. It is constantly travelling around us, yet we are so unaware of it. I slowly nodded my head in fascination. *How have I gone my whole life and not noticed the abundance of sounds that drift in waves around me?* I wasn't sure if I became aware of the sounds because I was in the present or whether awareness of the sounds helped me return to the present. I realised that I could use it as a pointer to help me come back to the present moment whenever I drifted and became overwhelmed by my own thoughts and emotions.

Now as I practiced meditation, I listened to all the sounds around me. Previously, I would ask my family to be quiet or meditate in an isolated area to ensure no distraction from noise.

When I meditated, I accepted and listened carefully to every subtle sound occurring around and within me. The faint ticking of the kitchen clock, the cars driving past my home, the birds chirping in the garden, the chattering of people walking past, sounds from the television, my children fighting in the next room ... I listened to every sound, accepting them as the external space accepts all.

This is true listening—all-inclusive. Listening, where we accept every sound we hear, rather than just concentrating on one noise. Listening where we don't discriminate, where we don't judge. This can also be applied when listening to someone speaking. Often, we don't listen to others when they are communicating with us. Often we are in our minds thinking about something, mostly trying to defend a mind-conceived point of view or are thinking and judging what they are saying. If we just became aware that we are listening, then we will hear and understand exactly what they are saying, even things that they haven't conveyed—the truth behind what they are saying or notice the tone or pauses in their speech.

Now when I talk to people, just by listening intently, I can have much more meaningful conversations. When I listen to my wife, I become aware and listen without interrupting and imposing my judgements. I allow her to let everything out, which is really what she wants. When I talk to my children and ask, 'How was your day today?' I listen as they sigh or bluntly say, 'Good.' I don't react to what they say. I just listen. I observe their expressions and allow them to have space rather than trying to make them

131

open, like I may have tried before. The amazing thing I also noticed is that when I'm communicating in the present, words just come to me. And the words that come out of my mouth are honest and genuine. It seems so natural, and the awkwardness I once felt when conversing seems to disappear.

When we become more present, not only does it enhance our sense of hearing, but all our senses. It's almost like all this time we've been travelling in a bubble, never really seeing, hearing, smelling, or touching. We notice sounds that are always there, but we never seemed to tune into the subtle sounds that travel within the space around us.

Eighteen

A Whole New World

Something has changed, and the effects ripple outwards.

Life had significantly changed. The weight that used to drag me down had disappeared. I also felt so much more alive; the world had become more vivid and colourful. It was as though I had been blindfolded for all those years; everything had been shadowed in shades of black and white and moved in perpetual sluggishness. Life was coming back to me. I had boundless energy instead of constant fatigue I used to experience nearly every day of my life. Previously, I would return home from work tired from a day of staring at the computer, listening to meetings, writing emails, and sitting in the pathetic Melbourne traffic. Now I returned home excited to see my family; excited to spend some time with myself, and excited for life.

*   *   *

One day, when I went for my afternoon coffee, I was truly able to appreciate the miracle of this new way of living—a life of awareness. It was as if all my sense perceptions became truly alive. A new kind of seeing, a new kind of listening, a new kind of smell. I listened, smelled and tasted with my whole being. Perhaps all my ten trillion cells were alive, full of joy, and working together as one. No longer under the pump. No longer under stress. No longer under the burden of constant compulsive thinking.

I looked around at the picturesque little café, with its wide windows and rustic brick walls, and for the first time, I looked at my coffee. Truly observed it, rather than just gulping it down. I noticed that Jackson, my favourite barista, was at work today. He makes coffee with so much effort, passion, and craftsmanship, from the frothy milky top with the swirling patterns to the strong, perfectly blended coffee beneath. The café was overwhelmed by a tangy sweetness from the fresh cakes on display and the morning special of blueberry pancakes. It was like this sudden explosion of stimuli for my brain; however, it wasn't overwhelming. Today I was not even phased by the cacophony of sounds that inundated my ears—the screaming child, the loud chatter from the café, the drum of heavy rain outside, the constant hum of cars and buses, clattering cutlery against plates, the ticking of the old master grandfather clock, or even the loud, explosive phone conversation that the man beside me was having. It all seemed to occur together, simultaneously. Despite the discord, they all had a place in the space, so I merely accepted everything—every single noise that occurred around me.

Sitting in the corner near the artsy brick wall, I enjoyed my extra hot latte in the warm atmosphere inside, while the weather outside was wet and freezing. Through the corner of my eyes, I saw a lady pushing a pram trying to enter the coffeeshop. She was desperately trying to protect herself and her child from the rain while opening the door. A young boy, perhaps aged around nine or ten, saw this woman struggling and rushed to let her in. The woman smiled at the boy and thanked him. The boy went back to where his parents sat. The parents seemed unaware of this act of kindness from their son, too busy staring at their phones. I looked around to see if anyone else in the shop had observed the incident. Most were glued to their phones. However, for once, I witnessed everything—every activity. I felt alive and aware—an all-inclusive awareness, which I call 360-degree awareness.

*   *   *

I practised my multiple pointers to help stay in the present throughout the day. Sometimes, interchanging from noticing my breath to noticing the space around me to asking my mind: *What are you thinking? Am I conscious in this moment?* Using various pointers seems to help me stay in the present for longer than using the same pointer, as, after a while of using the same thing, it becomes almost methodical and seems to have no effect in taming my mind. When I focus on my breath for a long period, I become used to the rhythm once again and lose myself in a flood of thoughts. Likewise, questioning my mind could become methodical after a time, where I am absently asking myself the question without awareness or a pause in my incessant thoughts.

Shifting between each of these pointers became an efficient way to stay in the present longer. The space between my thoughts was progressively increasing each day, and I felt that now I had witnessed this new wholesome way of life, I was even more determined to not go back.

Initially, when I was taken seriously ill in Perth, my mind would stir and ask: *Why? Why did it happen to me? What had I done to deserve this? Why me?* I constantly questioned the reason for my suffering after being diagnosed. It was unfair. I had lived a healthy life, tried to do the right thing. In hindsight, I began to accept it and realise that perhaps my experience of suffering was necessary—a blessing in disguise? I don't know. It may have happened for a reason, and I thankfully learned from it. It was a wake-up call in every sense of the word. As if the Divine Intelligence wanted me to wake up from the deep slumber. Maybe, the doctor's shocking verdict had come in the form of Divine intervention—the last chance to change, to become aware. A single fading line, waiting for me to grab on and transform, and I took it with everything that I had.

It is then that I realised that the challenges that life throws at us are learning opportunities; however, so many of us perceive these challenges to be negative, making us anxious and fearful in the face of crisis. Following that period of suffering, I was finally able to appreciate life for all the blessings that it had provided me and understand the true meaning of selfless love and kindness.

Experiencing intense suffering, such as a near-death experience or loss, can dissolve all our past baggage and accumulated conditioning. During the time of suffering, we may ask the questions, 'Why me? What did I do to deserve this?' However, once we overcome the challenge, we realise how much it changes and teaches us. Suffering helped reduce my mind-conceived self, which was full of arrogance, anger, jealousy, and insatiable ambition, and helped me break through the prison of conditioning in which I had locked myself. I found the true version of myself, the innocent child that I had once been. Everything happens for a reason; however, we don't see the big picture until the end. The whole ordeal taught me to have faith in this journey called life and to embrace each moment while we have it.

Now I am finally alive. I am attuned to life and free, and I am more accepting and forgiving. Previously, with the burden of my conditioning, I would have shouted at others, including my own children, when they made a mistake or deviated from what I thought was right. Now, I have realised that they are children and will learn as I have learned. I only hope that they don't have to go through the same intense suffering as I did. I hope they realise this truth sooner rather than later. Before the hospital episode, it was all about 'I am right, and all others are wrong. My wife is wrong. My children are wrong. I need to teach them.' And so, I went about correcting them. I felt angry and distressed about everything. This caused a lot of tension in the family.

Now, having woken up from a deep slumber, it was all about acceptance. When I began to correct myself as I realised my ignorance, my world changed. There was no longer the urge to correct others. I simply corrected myself. Even today, I am realising and correcting my ignorance as it arises. This is a work in progress. It is as if I am shining light on myself and cleaning out any conditioned behaviours, like cleaning up the cobwebs and keeping the room clean. This simple consciousness has transformed my world. I was asleep all those years and allowed the mind-conceived conditioned behaviours to overpower me and express themselves through me. Due to lack of awareness, I had allowed emotions like anger and frustration to overpower me. Now, with greater awareness, I consciously observe these emotions that try to overpower and act through me. This has been one significant change in my life for the better.

Due to this constant awareness, I could feel myself gaining control of my emotions. In the past, rage consumed me like a hungry fire. However, as soon as I felt the flicker of anger, I would immediately acknowledge that I was angry, and the space within me would help the anger subside. In the past, I didn't even realise that the heat of anger had overcome me. By the time I realised, the roaring flames would have already left a trail of destruction. The deeper the awareness that I gave to myself, the less likely it was that these conditioned behaviours impacted me—or rather, I stopped giving them the power that they were seeking.

This constant observation and attentiveness—in other words, conscious awareness—of thoughts and feelings when they arise, whether we are at work or at home, is the secret to a fulfilling and peaceful life. It is the simple equation to ending our suffering and living a life free from anger, fear, stress, ego, anxiety, hatred, jealousy, and violence. It is also the way out of ignorance—a state in which we can fully forgive. Forgive others for their ignorance. For being unmindful and allowing their conditioned behaviours to overtake them and be expressed through them.

Using my various pointers of training for my mind to become more aware, the years of conditioning have slowly eased their grip on me. Now I live in a place where I am comfortable and confident —a place where I am loved, a place where I am one with the world. I am finally experiencing real contentment, real love, and real joy. In other words, I am in sync with life. My emotions and feelings are not dependent on anything, and nor do they control me. I allow myself to be content, to show unconditional love, to be joyful. No longer do I have mornings where I wake up grudgingly, despairing at the mediocrity of the day. Every morning becomes another way to welcome life and have new experiences. Every day is a new opportunity to learn and bring warmth to the lives of others.

My question, though, is, 'Do we all have to go through intense suffering to realise our true selves?' Is there another way to bring awareness to people so we can finally live joyful and fulfilling lives?

Nineteen

Finding a Lost Friend

Freedom arises from the simple,
effortless practice of being aware.

There is a pure, childlike innocence lying deep within all of us. At some stage in our lives, we desperately seek it. We look for it everywhere—through others, experiences, books, religion, temples, mosques, churches, travelling to the Himalayas ... We search for it everywhere. Hoping to find that missing piece, that missing part of us, hoping that someday we will feel complete. The irony doesn't fail to surprise me. The desperate seeker is nothing but mind-conceived. However, when the mind-conceived seeker in us surrenders, there it is. We see clearly what we've been looking for—our 'true self'. We look everywhere for something that was always hiding within us, waiting for us to recognise it. It is akin to desperately looking for your reading glasses only to find that they were firmly on your head the whole time. All these years, our conditioned minds have kept our true innocence dormant, preventing us from expressing it.

For most of my life, I had felt like something was missing, like I was incomplete. Over time I believed that it was because I needed to make a name for myself, find my identity in society. I needed to prove to others that I could achieve great things in life. I was driven by insatiable ambition and, as a result, became selfish and egocentric. Everything was about me and the wellbeing of my immediate family. However, even as I climbed the ladder of success, I felt no satisfaction as I stepped up each rung. It felt like I was losing more of myself the higher I climbed. That feeling of incompleteness was always present during my adult life, and I attempted to fill it with tangible things. Yet, it wasn't until now that I felt like I was whole again.

After all these years of searching, my self-realisation has finally shed light on the most profound truth. A truth that gave me the courage to face my own 'conditioned self' and free my hidden 'true self'. This feeling of liberation cannot be expressed in words, and I struggle to find a word to describe it, as nothing seems to give it the justice it deserves.

I imagine a beautiful tree flourishing under the sun. One day a small weed took shelter beneath its protective branches. The manipulative plant then siphoned nutrients away from the tree. Growing bigger off the tree's nutrients, the parasitic plant grew and overwhelmed the tree. The parasitic plant then flourished and thrived as the beautiful tree withered away due to constant stress and lack of nutrients. Eventually, the parasite had full control, and the host plant had become a slave to the parasite, providing it with nutrients and giving it the support to dominate. This is the power of the mind.

I realised that this had been the reason that I had been struggling all these years. My parasitic mind-conceived 'self', or the conditioned 'self', had taken complete control. I had lost control of my mind, and it was feeding on my emotions, thoughts and energy. It was even feeding on my health, almost killing me with its destructive intentions. I had been completely unaware of the parasite, with the mind-conceived conditioned 'self' gaining strength and dominating me. Now, after years of suffering, I am learning to become more aware and to cut down the growing parasite before it overwhelms me.

The simple and effortless practice of being aware, just being conscious, was all it took to realise the conditioning of my mind, to become fully aware of its activity, its intentions to dominate and take away my control of myself. When I am aware, at that moment I have full control of myself, and my mind stays away. At that moment, the inner conflict, the unwanted mind noise, is gone, and there is peace within. I am at peace with my own true being. My true form begins to express itself fully and unconditional love comes into being. There's a sense of connectedness with every other being. I begin to see myself in others. We are all just one energy but in different forms. *How can I then ever hurt any other form? How can I feel anger, jealousy or hate towards another person?* A feeling of oneness overwhelms me, and I feel a sense of connectedness with the world. Like the last missing puzzle piece is finally put in place. A perfect serenity.

Pure energy all around. A feeling of responsiveness and aliveness. There is joy, beauty, and benevolence all around. This is what I call flourishing and fully flowering. However, the mind parasite may not allow me to be in that form for too long. It constantly tries to come back and gain control. I need to be more deeply aware of this mind trying to take control.

My practice these days is to bring that awareness within me, moment to moment, and be fully aware of the parasitic mind overwhelming me. The practice is simple and effortless. I don't condemn the mind; I don't try to control it. I just let my mind wander. I accept that it is the mind's nature to wander. I notice it coming in and imposing its destructive thoughts and judgements onto me. I don't identify with it. I am fully aware of where it's taking me—this conscious awareness is the key.

After all, the mind is not completely bad. It's an essential tool for our survival. It has a limited but very important role in our lives. It is how we make use of the mind that is most important. In a metaphorical sense, I consider the mind as a torchlight in the darkness. Most of the time the torchlight is with me in the present to shine light on the path closest to me. However, whenever I want to look back (such as into the past) I can use it to shed light behind me. Whenever I wish to see a in front of me (such as into the future), I can shine the light ahead of me. It is always at my beck and call, and so is the mind. A useful tool indeed, if used wisely. However, for us to use our mind wisely we need deeper consciousness and awareness.

Acquired knowledge is required for our survival within

society. Knowledge about geography, maths, sciences and even our own identity is necessary for us to function as members of society. However, if we want to flourish and thrive, without the influence of debilitating thoughts and emotions, we must go beyond the mind's intellect. We must regain conscious awareness over our mind to prevent it from taking control.

I imagine that training our mind is like training a new puppy. New puppies are curious, wandering and out of control when improperly trained. In this metaphor, the leash is the awareness and the puppy is the mind. The more we allow the puppy to wander, the more confusion it can cause. The sooner we pull the puppy back with the help of the leash, the better it is for us. The more we notice that our dog is wandering and the more often we are aware, attentive and try to bring it back, the sooner the dog will know not to wander anymore. After a while, we don't require the leash to tame the puppy. Likewise, the more we notice that our mind is wandering away into the past or future, and the more often we try to bring it back to the present, the sooner our mind (of its own volition) will come to know that it is futile to wander and the less anxious and stressed we will be in life. Initially, we may need to constantly remind ourselves to be aware or mindful. But over a period, with practice, we will no longer require a reminder to bring ourselves back to the present. Being in that awareness becomes an effortless way of being for us.

At times, I was anxious about losing my awareness. I can lose it for up to a few minutes and sometimes for hours. The mind takes control all over again, plunging me into my old,

145

conditioned self. I used to be frustrated, overcome by confusion and anger at having lost myself to the mind. Then, with practice, I realised that the feeling of anxiety was also mind-conceived. Hence, I was still trapped. So, I became aware of that feeling. I became aware of the anxiety that I felt about being taken over by the mind. I normalised it and became comfortable with it. Just the mere practice of acceptance would immediately bring me back to that moment of awareness and presence. Whenever I feel anxious, stressed, angry, or annoyed, I realise that I have moved away from being in that state of awareness and the mind has taken control. This awareness brings me back to the present, to my true form.

Through self-discovery, I have realised that being in a state of awareness is our primordial state. It's our home, where we truly belong. Within this state, we can finally live prosperous and fulfilling lives.

I regained a connection. I regained my lost connection with Intelligence.

Twenty

The Art of Conscious Balance

Everything happens for us. Everything aligns itself for us.
There is no more struggle.

A s children, we were born into that state of awareness, as unconditioned, uncorrupted beings. However, during our upbringing, we become unaware and allow the mind parasite to take control.

When the mind is in control, it likes to assume that it is all-knowing and powerful. In our mind-conditioned state we may often hear ourselves say, 'I know,' and, 'I understand.' *Yet, what do we really know? And what do we really understand? Where does this knowing coming from?*

Everything that we know and supposedly understand is an accumulation of knowledge that's been acquired from the past. I call this knowledge the 'intellect'. A collection of experiences, memories, and information from our past, stored within our brains. To 'know' or 'understand' anything, our brain recollects and draws upon past information and knowledge to provide answers. Yet, the information we have stored may be limited, incomplete, misinformed, and, at best, outdated. The intellect is not born out of true understanding or learning; it is a remnant of information passed down. It should not be the only form of learning and awareness that we follow. So, while some intellect is required to function efficiently in society, too much emphasis on acquired knowledge can prevent us from tapping into the unlimited Universal Intelligence.

Essentially, the intellect is mind-conceived and driven by thought. However, Intelligence is pure, true and born through Divine Energy. Intelligence has all the answers we ever need in life; however, we just need to listen and embrace its power.

I've encountered its power many times throughout my life but dismissed it as luck. However, I have felt that luck doesn't just occur. It's a consequence of 'Divine Intervention'.

There was one moment when I drove home after a long day at work. Cars were packed back-to-back on the road. When the lights turned green, I drove forwards, following the concrete truck in front of me. The truck suddenly came to a standstill, and I quickly stamped on the brake. Due to space in between, I had ample time to stop, but at that moment, I looked in my rear-view mirror to see a blue car hurtling towards me. I had no time to react or even think as the car smashed into mine, forcing me forwards with its momentum.

I watched in shock as my car careened towards the back of the truck. In that second, my brain went blank, and I knew I would crash the front of my car into the truck. By some instinctive power, I slammed my foot on the brake with all my force. The car screamed to a nerve-racking stop, mere millimetres from the back of the truck. If I had moved the slightest bit in my seat, my car would have collided with the truck. All I remember was feeling stunned and sitting there for what felt like minutes until my heart stopped pounding, and my fingers stopped shaking. Within moments, the traffic eased, and the truck moved forwards, driving along the road as if nothing had happened. I sat there in my car, unable to move, think, or even check to see if everything was alright. I was startled out of my reverie when a person knocked on my window. It was a paramedic. Apparently, there was an ambulance stuck in the traffic behind me. They were going back to their base after attending to an emergency call. The paramedic did some initial tests and checked for my vitals. They told me that everything was normal, and I was fine to go. *How did that happen? How was help exactly where I needed it? I have no idea—the power of the Intelligence is unfathomable.*

Some might call that instinctive action 'luck'. But to this day, I don't know what possessed me to step on the brake. I don't know how I had stopped in time to not hit the truck. It wasn't an action that my brain had controlled. At that moment, I had no previous memory or information that could have helped me. My mind was lost on what to do, so my intellect had surrendered, and my thoughts vanished. In that space, the Intelligence was able to act through me, guiding me and saving me.

Miracles occur when intelligence prevails. There may have

been moments in your own life where you have been completely lost. But somehow, miraculously, everything falls into place. *How does it happen?*

When there is thought (intellect), there is no space. As a result, there is no space for Intelligence to act through us, so we struggle. When we are fully aware, thought activity surrenders, creating a beautiful space within us, paving the way for the Intelligence to flow through us. In that space, everything happens for us as if we are in sync with life. Everything aligns itself for us. An action that is complete, creative, and apt, manifests itself. There are no more struggles. The mind realises its limitations and surrenders. We no longer have to concentrate and resist the temptation of distraction. The brain is fresh and rejuvenated, with plenty of energy and space for creative action—allowing the abundant, unlimited and natural Intelligence to flow through.

It is within this space where anything innovative and new can be discovered. When our minds are burdened by the baggage of thoughts, memories, and judgements, nothing further can be found, as the old inhibits us from seeing clearly. However, when our mind is still, we are opening ourselves to something new, as the present moment is continually fresh. It is within this space of peace that outstanding art, music, films, writing, inventions and initiatives are created.

True creativity and innovation are born in the space of Intelligence because it is new and inspiring.

And while we are within this space of peace, our limited intellect that we've been collecting all our life is no longer our only source of information. We tap into a profound source, an unlimited source that has all the answers. A source that is true and pure and forever eternal—a source that I call 'Intelligence', a Divine energy that guides and nurtures us. It is present within everything. In every living cell, in the floating dust particles and in the person sitting beside you. It is the Divine energy that circulates throughout the universe. The space in which everything happens. For all those years since birth, we resist and block the guidance of the Divine Intelligence. We decided that we don't need the help and that we could take care of ourselves. However, it was always watching us, waiting for that moment when we would open ourselves to its brilliant guidance.

Imagine that the Intellect is like a candle flame providing light in a dark room. In the stark darkness, the flickering light gives brightness to the room. However, if the intellect envisions itself to be supreme and powerful, it is mistaken. We only need to open the doors and windows and let the sun's light into the room to see that the power of the candlelight is easily diminished. Candlelight surrenders in the presence of the expansive power of the sun. Nothing compares to the abundant and generous power of the Intelligence, the Divine.

Our mind (intellect) considers itself powerful and supreme; put on a pedestal to make major life decisions. We may have been conditioned to position it this way. As a result, we allow it to hijack us. Often, we don't even question the decisions that

151

it makes for us. This places serious limitations on our inner evolution.

I realised that the Intelligence comes into being when the intellect (acquired knowledge) surrenders and says, 'I do not know'. In other words, when the 'conditioned self', with its arrogance of 'knowing', is recognised or surrenders, a space of creativity that surpasses the level of the mind comes into being. However, our mind is not usually comfortable with this space of 'not knowing'. If we can be comfortable with our humility and insignificance, by recognising or becoming aware of the uneasiness of the mind, we may be able to open ourselves to the possibility of that profound, pure and unlimited knowing.

You, too, may have already had an experience where the Intelligence intervenes most unexpectedly, moments when you felt helpless and completely lost with no hope or direction. And suddenly, an opportunity or support arises from somewhere. Sometimes when something miraculous happens, we can't comprehend how it all fell into place. When we allow the Intelligence to guide us, our lives will be fulfilling and complete.

*   *   *

Over my years of self-discovery, I realised an essential quality of the mind. We cannot force the mind to surrender and become silent. We cannot force our thoughts to stop or force our emotions to cease. I used to force my mind to turn off, fighting against the thoughts that bombarded me. I would sit there silently, willing my mind to *stop, stop thinking, stop thinking*... a futile, repetitive chant. It was tedious and exhausting, and I used to come out of these mindfulness sessions feeling even more conflict and confusion. It wasn't until one winter evening, when I went for a run, that I began to understand.

It was a particularly crisp winter's day, and the wind had a ferocious bite. The sky had been overcast most of the day. But towards the end of the day, it began to clear, giving way to small patches of bright blue. As I ran in the fading light, I noticed my shadow in my periphery, cast by the streetlights. I ran around my block and made my way towards my house and there it was, my shadow still following me. No matter how far I ran or how fast, there it was, following me. That's when it struck me. Trying to control my mind was like running away from the fear of my own shadow. You cannot win. The mind must realise its limitations and surrender on its own, thus paving the way for unlimited intelligence to flow through. This can come out only by being totally self-aware, conscious, and mindful.

The intellect (our mind) is essential for functioning effectively within society. However, if we want to fully evolve, flourish and flower as a being, we need to embrace a greater power—the Universal Intelligence.

Both the intellect and the power of the Universal Intelligence are at our disposal. As a habit we have made use of just the limited intellect, ignoring the unlimited power of the Universal intelligence. Therefore, we struggle.

With conscious awareness, we will know when to use the

intellect and when to keep it away, paving way for the profound Universal intelligence to act through us.

This is what I call the Art of Conscious Balance. Knowing how to balance the intellect and Intelligence. This balance comes with practice and deeper self-awareness. Over time our awareness and ability to balance between the intellect and the Intelligence becomes second nature to us. When we embrace the profound power of Universal Intelligence, we can tune into and elevate ourselves to a different realm within life. We become better. We are grounded. We operate efficiently. We achieve Clarity and become Conscious, Creative, Calm, Compassionate and Connected beings.

Finding this balance has taken me immense time and experience. But the miraculous thing is that this transformation is a single-step process. The moment the intellect is kept away—when the mind becomes quiet with our deeper awareness—it allows the intelligence to act through. It's that simple.

Twenty-One

The Seeds of Change

The change began with me.

During a normal working afternoon, I walked into a room full of staff for the monthly sales meeting. People sat on chairs arranged around a long mahogany table. I entered, smiling at my colleagues, and sat in an empty chair beside Albert, an elderly man who had been in the company for fifteen years. Most waited silently, while some talked to each other in clipped sentences.

I smiled at Albert, who looked a bit forlorn and tired. 'How's everything going, Albert? Everything going well with the family?'

Albert looked at me in surprise. We had worked together for a couple of years yet we rarely conversed about our personal lives. Usually, I would walk into the meetings, take my seat, and scan through my phone, looking at emails. I tried not to make eye contact or conversation with anyone. What was the point? We were all working. Small talk wasn't interesting. But I had changed.

Albert turned towards me with a tentative smile. 'Not bad,

155

Santosh. The family's okay. Everyone's busy with their own things.'

Remembering something I'd overheard around the office, I asked, 'How's your daughter? I heard that she got married recently. That must've been exciting?'

Albert beamed. He seemed surprised that I was interested. 'Oh, it was great. She was so happy! It was a wonderful day. We held it in Berwick, at the Wilson Botanical Gardens. My wife was really happy because that's where we got married.'

I smiled—his happiness was infectious.

Suddenly, everyone quietened as the meeting commenced. I had always detested these meetings. They were dangerous, competitive, and threatening, yet I had used them as an opportunity to prove myself worthy. I used to try too hard, competing against everyone else, proving to them I had done the best, that I knew everything. I had been ruthless, putting other team members down while boasting about my own team's performance and the other team's loss. Yet today, as people argued and proved themselves across the table, I merely listened. I watched my team members, some with their claws ready and eyes glaring. As the room filled with hostility and competitiveness, I tried to maintain the presence in my mind. By bringing awareness to my breathing I was able to remain calm. For the first time at work, I felt grounded. I didn't have to prove my worth to anyone, I didn't have to demean anyone, and I didn't have to become an insatiable monster greedy for success. I just accepted everything—listening and watching and trying not to judge anyone. An invisible barrier had lifted.

When my boss, John, sighed, I began to think. For an hour, I listened to Maria argue with Havier about ways to increase sales without compromising customer convenience. They both threw ideas back and forth, asserting that their own plan was better. John looked torn; I also knew that he was worried about his daughter, who had just undergone surgery and was recovering in hospital. This meeting was not helping him, nor the others in the room. As I sat there watching the people I had been working with for years, an idea popped into my head. If we found a way to consolidate all our shipments from our suppliers, we could reduce our shipping costs. Especially as many of our suppliers were from the US. I decided to suggest this idea, hoping that rather than an argument, we could obtain a solution.

I stood up, immediately obliging the others in the room to be silent. My ruthlessness in meetings was known to everyone. My voice rang through the room. 'Apologies for the interruption Maria, but there might be another way. I don't know if this will work, but it's just a suggestion. How about if we consolidate all the shipments from California each week and then send them to the customers? Reducing shipping costs, which would increase profits. What do you all think?'

John looked down, his brows furrowed, while Maria and Havier peered at each other. Sitting down, I resumed my careful observation of my mind. I didn't know where my patience had come from, nor the courteous attitude, but it felt more enjoyable than the tiring aggressive response I would have gone for before.

John stood. 'Okay, thank you, Santosh, this is something we could look into. Maria, I want you to see how much more profitable this would be, and Havier, I would like you to talk to your contacts and see if this can be initiated. Now, I've spent too much time in this room, and I'd like to spend the rest of the night with my family, so that's all for today.'

Slowly, everyone got up and filed out of the room. There were quiet murmurs as people looked at me and John. I walked out with Albert. He told me that he would be spending his weekend with his young grandson playing mini-golf. I laughed, telling him about my son's catastrophic fifth birthday party at a mini-golf place.

'Santosh, could I talk to you for a moment?' John called out as I reached the door. Patting Albert on the arm in goodbye, I approached John.

'Hi John, anything wrong?'

'No, not at all. I've been watching you ... I've noticed something different about you. Something has changed. You're more grounded, more patient. I'm impressed, you handled that meeting very well, and you proved to be a great team player.'

I nodded at him, smiling. 'Thanks, John. Yeah, I feel different. How's your daughter doing? My wife was asking if she's out of the hospital.'

He smiled. 'She is doing much better. It turns out she just had a cyst, which they've removed. She can go back to playing soccer.'

I clapped him on the back. 'That's great! Kids are so resilient. I was worried when my daughter fell from the monkey bars at her school and broke her arm at the growth plate. They said her arm might not grow, as the growth plate is crucial for the growth of the bone, but she's perfectly fine now. Her arm grew, and not a single thing went wrong.' I chuckled. 'It's definitely been tough.'

*   *   *

My family also noticed a change. When my wife was in the kitchen making breakfast before work, I would walk in with a broad smile, wishing everyone a good morning, and she would peer at me with an incredulous look. She was used to a grumpy and distant version of her husband in the mornings.

So often, we wake up dreading the day ahead, as it's just a tireless continuation of the previous day. I was the same. My mind used to churn with thoughts of what I had to do throughout the day, so I was always rushing to get through the morning and get to work. Now mornings were the best part of my day. Everything just seems like another opportunity to start over. A new day. A new world. A new way of living.

One day she surprised me when we were drinking our morning tea together. I was quietly enjoying the warm tea watching the steam swirling in the cold winter air. I noticed her watching me curiously. 'You've changed,' she said. 'Something has changed within you. You've become a different person, someone better.'

I smiled. My wife was the only person who truly knew me, and it made me proud that she had noticed the significant change within me. She had helped me through my worst and most

159

terrifying moments. In fact, she had shown me the meaning of unconditional love and patience. She had transformed me with her compassion and shown me that there was a different way of life. She inspired me to explore my self-inquiry. It was then that I realised how important it is to have loved ones in your life. To have people who care for us, challenge us, and help us grow. Many people attempt to distance themselves from others as they delve into self-discovery. They seek solitude and try to remove themselves from the confusion of society and relationships. Whereas I came to realise that society and relationships, although tedious, challenged me and helped me to become aware of my own mind-conceived baggage. Being a husband, a son, a sibling, and a father are all difficult roles, most likely a source of stress and confusion for the old Santosh. However, I saw that these roles provided me with an opportunity to learn to grow and interact with the world.

My daughter was growing and developing through her teenage phase. She had always been a happy, lively kid; however, as she went through this phase, she started changing. She became more reclusive, agitated, stubborn, and seemed to revel in infuriating her mother. She wouldn't listen to anyone and became good at talking back. It was hard to manage. It really tested my patience, and it angered me when she poked at my ego. However, through self-awareness, I attempted to manage my anger. It was difficult, so difficult. She knew how to press our buttons. She reminded me of my previous self, and it scared me to see my own anger and stubbornness on her face.

There were times when I acted in anger, exacerbating her anger and the situation. But in some rare moments, I was able to bring peace within myself, allowing myself to be patient with her anger and frustration. I began to understand her in a way that would not have been possible if not for my change. I was able to empathise and remember my own confusing transition into adulthood. I remembered my lack of support and how lost I had felt back then. I didn't want her to go through the same plight. I wanted her to feel supported, comfortable, and have a safe place to talk and grow. With that awareness, instead of retaliating and arguing with her, I just listened and gave her some space. I didn't push or pry, but I let her feel like she could talk to us while letting her explore whatever emotions she was feeling. My wife found this frustratingly difficult. Despite her innate ability to be patient and compassionate, she was, by nature, someone who needed to fix things. And seeing her daughter unhappy made her frustrated. I tried to reason with my wife, explaining that our daughter needed space and that she was just going to get madder if she intervened. This just made my wife more irritated. So, I decided that if I couldn't change either of them, I would just accept them. I would remain calm and grounded and bring presence in myself.

It wasn't until years later that my wife explained that she had watched the way I had been with my daughter and began to understand. My wife saw how my calmness and understanding had changed our daughter, how she would calm down in the face of my mellow composure. How our daughter became more open with me and slowly more comfortable with herself. My wife explained that she had learned from me to be patient with our daughter, which helped transform their relationship.

That's when I began to realise that just by changing myself, I could make a significant impact on those around me. I had initially tried to change everyone else, helping them understand what I had learned through my self-discovery. I tried to change my daughter, telling her how to behave, to observe her thoughts, to become more present—but it didn't work. Likewise, when I tried to change my wife, she had grown frustrated. However, just by changing the way I acted and behaved, I was able to significantly affect the lives of those I loved. This was my biggest accomplishment. This was the most powerful transformation I could ever hope for. I may not be able to change the world, not even my family, but I could change myself. I had a choice.

*   *   *

One afternoon at my favourite coffee shop, I was once again forced to make a choice between my conditioned mind and my newfound awareness. I had ordered my coffee and walked over to a comfortable chair in the corner. As I was making myself comfortable, from the corner of my eye, I saw someone sitting across from me whom I vaguely remembered. My mind immediately went to work, scanning through my memory to recognise the individual. Within seconds, memories projected into my mind, and I immediately recognised him as Scott, an old work colleague. We used to work together at the same firm over twelve years ago. He was one of those people who had been ambitious and arrogant, much like how I had been. He was ruthless when it came to business and had caused me great strife when I had started at the firm. He demeaned everyone to prove his worth, and we had many conflicting experiences together. Upon seeing him, I felt my heart rate increase in anger, and I had a sudden urge to leave immediately before he saw me. I really did not want to be reacquainted with Scott. However, in that moment, my practised consciousness intervened. I re-centred myself, coming back into the present as my mind and its unpleasant memories faded into the background. From my hidden place in the corner, I took a moment to look at my old colleague. I noticed the fine lines on his face and the greying hair. He had aged considerably, and with it, I noticed that he had lost the aggression that used to line his face. I noticed the softness in his eyes as he spoke to the waiter at the counter. He looked completely different. Maybe it was unfair of me to judge him based on his past, when he may have changed considerably in the last twelve years. Ignoring the intervening commands of my negative mind, I rose and walked towards him at the front of the café. Standing behind him, I tapped his shoulder and he turned in surprise. He immediately recognised me.

'Hi Scott, do you remember me?'

'Santosh!' he exclaimed in surprise.

'Of course! It's been a very long time. How have you been?' I smiled, enthused by his transformation. I had never seen him smile throughout our time working together. As we reacquainted, I learned much about Scott and his life over the past twelve years. He had indeed undergone a transformation in that time, much like myself. He had worked in the corporate world and maintained his ruthless persona. However, over time, he became tired and exhausted by the success-driven life. He had retired early and lived in an isolated town called Paynesville, in the Gippsland region of Australia. He led a quiet life with his wife, spending his time sailing, fishing and volunteering as a representative of the small town with the local council. He enjoyed his quiet and peaceful life near the water and was much happier. After sharing our stories and laughing over the changes in our lives, we went our separate ways with the promise to keep in touch. As I left, Scott called out to me. I turned in surprise, wondering if I had left something behind.

'Santosh, before I forget ... I want to use this opportunity to apologise for how I used to be. I know that it must not have been easy for you to work with me. I made it hard for you at the company when you started, and you didn't deserve that.'

I smiled at him, shaking his extended hand in gratitude and forgiveness. 'It's all old baggage, there's nothing to apologise for'. I leaned in for hug, and we embraced as old friends.

As I drove home, I smiled, glad that I had accepted the choice to ignore my conditioned mind but instead to talk to Scott. I felt immense peace that the relationship had been mended and my veil of conditioning against him had been lifted. What a beautiful being he turned out to be!

We tend to look at everyone through the glass of our past. Our mind goes back into the past experiences, stored in our memory, and we often look at people in our lives, including our partner, children, parents, and friends, through the mental images of the past. We look at them with that judgement that we have about each of them and therefore we do not see them as they are in the present moment. Scott had changed. Changed for good. But I was looking at him through the baggage of the past.

*   *   *

Many people aspire to make huge changes. They wish to leave the world, having made an impact. But as we grow older, the magnitude of this dream wears us down. The world is a complex place, marred by violence, poverty, wars, politics, and so much hardship. Millions of people live their lives in constant struggle, struggling to survive against every force that threatens to kill them—poverty, corruption, viruses, bacteria, hospitals. I am specifically referring to the COVID-19 pandemic as I write this book. Humanity has been severely impacted by the current pandemic. Many millions have lost their lives, and many are still suffering. But despite all this darkness, human life has prevailed. Despite generations of people and millennia of struggle, humanity has remained strong. As if the Intelligence knows that we have strength. Strength together. Changing the world is no easy feat for anyone, let alone one person. Throughout history, we have learned that although possible, forcing people to change or conform to specific ideals can be detrimental. We do not possess the capacity to force others to transform. We may not be able to change the circumstances or the things that we encounter in life. The only thing that we can change is ourselves. We can acquire control over ourselves to ensure that we are the people that we want to be. As Gandhi eloquently said, 'Be the change you wish to see in the world.' This is one of the most powerful things that we need to acknowledge. By undergoing transformation, we possess the ability to change our own lives. We cannot change our circumstances; however, we can change how we perceive and react to the situations that we face. Likewise, we can't change the people around us. However, we can change the way we judge and respond to the people around us.

This is exactly what my self-discovery taught me, and it is one of the most powerful things that I have ever witnessed. My world changed because I underwent a transformation. My clouded vision was cleansed, giving me clarity. A world that once looked small, cold, ruthless and desolate, became bigger, warmer, welcoming and full of life. My outlook towards the world changed and, as a result, the way I interacted with the world changed. When we embrace the world, the world can't help but welcome us with the same enthusiasm and optimism.

Opportunities suddenly became available in my life. I had supportive people around me who were willing to help me grow. I had faith in life and in myself, this innate belief that everything would be okay if I stayed grounded and connected with the Intelligence. I had faith that the Intelligence would guide me and give me all that I needed to grow.

Twenty-two

Forgiveness—The Ultimate Act of Love

Grateful For Everything

After a long struggle and success-driven madness, I went for a well-deserved vacation to my motherland. As I sat on the plane, staring out of the window at the glittering night sky around me, I felt utterly at peace. The cruising plane flew through the vast sky while the hundreds of people on board slept peacefully. But it wasn't just the relaxed atmosphere that made me so serene; it was that inner peace within me, almost like a still pool of water, creating a perfectly clear reflection of the world around it. I felt lighter, less anxious, and I hadn't felt an overwhelming sense of emotions taking over in a long time. I was finally able to feel and live in the moment. Rather than worry about the past and future, I was in the present. For that glorious moment, I witnessed and marvelled at the beautiful starry night outside my window as the rest of the world slept around me.

The flight landed in the dusty, hot city of Bangalore, now renamed Bengaluru. I watched as we descended from the vastness of the sky to the bustling, colourful city below. Tall buildings were silhouetted against the rising sun as I neared the city I used to call home before leaving India.

After staying in Bengaluru for a couple of days, meeting some old friends and seeing how much the city had changed, I was due to leave for Kerala that evening. Packing my suitcase, I made my way out of the hotel to where a taxi waited for me. The taxi took me to Bengaluru City Junction railway station. The traffic throughout Bengaluru was atrocious, and I was glad that I had left early as the ten-kilometre trip took over forty minutes. When I reached the train station, I made my way to the platform where the long passenger train waited. Hauling my suitcase and bags inside, I found my seat inside my carriage. It was empty, although I knew the spaces would fill up as the train stopped at each station on its way south. Putting my suitcases beneath my seat, I laid out my sheets on the seat, which converted into a bed. Tired from my travel, I sat down and stared out between the window's bars. The sky had darkened, and the train rattled rapidly across the lush green terrain. I watched in awe as we passed the city with its abundance of light and noise and headed towards the city's quiet outskirts. Small houses were clustered in remote areas; tiny lights illuminating the rural villages. Children ran across the dry sandy plains towards their warm homes for dinner. I used to be one of them, watching the train travelling in the distance, wondering who was on it, where they were travelling. Back then, I wanted to see the world. I wanted to grow up, become something, someone. I was constantly seeking the next adventure.

As I sat in the quietness of the sleeping train, I felt at home. There was no longer a need to ask the question, 'What's next?' I was comfortable and content in the now. I was grateful to be breathing again. To feel the beauty all around. I was blessed with a second lease of life. What more could I ask for? I had been on the verge of death, with no hope and no meaning in my life. All those years, I had lived in resentment, resentment that I was alone and that no one supported me. However, when it really mattered, I had a whole village to support me, and I was eternally grateful. When I finally realised this absolute truth, I cried. I hadn't cried in years, not since my diagnosis. But tears of gratitude, of innocence, overwhelmed me as I thought of the unconditional love I had been given. Love that I had neglected and taken for granted.

I became aware of my gratitude for all those that had supported and helped me—and I went back to everyone I had hurt in the past and asked for forgiveness.

I have come to realise that only when we are in the present, when we are that space of peace, can we really ask for forgiveness. When we are grounded, we become more aware of our behaviours and emotions, and have greater acceptance for our mistakes. Thus, we can overcome our ego and ask for forgiveness. Likewise, when we are mindful, we are at peace with ourselves and can show patience to forgive others. Looking back through history, many enlightened beings have shown unconditional love through forgiveness—'Forgive them for they know not what they do,' said Jesus as he was dying on the cross. When we are present, the individual's past dissolves, allowing us to forgive and forget.

I wanted my parents to know how much I appreciated and loved them. I wanted them to know that whatever words or actions I had inflicted upon them had been born out of ignorance and for that, I was profoundly sorry. The hardest and most valuable of these apologies was my apology to my father.

All my life, I had taken my father's love for granted. Being an Indian Air Force man, he was stoic and rarely showed emotion. As a child, I had been afraid of him, especially his domineering personality. He raised us with strict discipline and seemed unable to show love in the straightforward way children crave. He was tough on me. I was the oldest but also the most reckless of his three children. There were times when I would come home from hours of playing with my friends to my furious father. I didn't know what had made him so angry and I still don't. Maybe it was the constant playing and fooling around, or perhaps it was something to do with him. As a child, my innocence was still intact, and I would go to my father and apologise. I didn't know what I had done wrong, but I respected my father, so I apologised for whatever I had done to upset him.

My apology resulted in my father's anger dissipating and him putting an arm around my shoulders to give me a small hug. Everything was fine again. I often wondered where my innocence had gone and why I couldn't just say sorry as an adult. My ego always held me back. I caused a lot of anguish to my father, especially growing up. In a sense, I was rebelling. I wanted to prove to him that I was independent and capable. I contradicted everything he tried to tell me, my arrogance always resisting his advice. There was an incident when he tried to reason with me when I spat out that I didn't need his advice anymore. That I could decide by myself. He had paused, and his face had frozen. He looked as if I had slapped him. His eyes glistened, and in that moment, I wanted to take those words back, to tell him I didn't mean it. But I just stood there heartlessly, before he turned and walked away.

Now I could recognise my father's love. He showed it in his own way, but he was loving all the same. He always protected and looked out for his family and raised his three children with spirit. He was a loving grandfather who doted on his baby grandchildren. He was still the same father who always looked out for me, raised me to be strong, confident, independent. The man who fought for my education and made me the successful man I am today. He had done the best he could and I was so grateful. He was always there for me when I needed it most. If I could be a fraction of the man and father he had been, I would be proud. Fortunately, I was able to tell him how much I loved him.

My mother had so much love for her children, but even today, she would say she doesn't know how to express it and always feels guilty about it. I noticed my grandmother was the same and didn't show any affection towards my mother. I often wonder how we as children mechanically imbibe some of these behaviours from our parents or grandparents and unconsciously use them in our own life. As children, we got used to the fact that my mother had lots of love but seldom expressed it.

When I finally reached home the next afternoon, I was greeted by my father waiting at the platform. He was early, always punctual from years of discipline at the Indian Air Force. He welcomed me warmly, towering over me as he was taller than me, about 6ft2. He gave me a quick hug and took my hand luggage as I wheeled my suitcase towards the taxi.

*   *   *

One evening, I sat with my father on verandah of our house. It was a warm evening, but the cool breeze dampened the stifling humidity. A broad, arching hibiscus tree spread towards the sitting area. I leaned back against the cool stone pillar while my father sat in his wooden lazy chair. His eyes were closed as he enjoyed his favourite part of the day. The smell of roasting cumin seeds drifted in the air and the sound of crackling dry chillies followed. I relaxed, listening to my mother cooking in the kitchen and my father's slow breathing on that warm, spring evening. Within moments, as if on cue, my mother walked onto the verandah carrying a tray of steaming, golden tea and a plate of spicy snacks.

My father sat up, hungrily taking a cup of tea and a snack. My mother sat down next to my father. I tentatively sipped my hot tea. And so, we sat there quietly in the cool breeze, enjoying each other's company. As the light waned, we found ourselves talking—just casual conversation, about anything and everything. We spoke about the old days, when we used to live in Karaikudi in the state of Tamil Nadu. My mum remembered when my brother and I got into a fight, and I threw a plate at his head. We laughed, but we all remembered the scary incident. Thankfully, I hadn't thrown that hard, but my brother needed stitches for the gash on his forehead. He uses it to this day, telling my kids about the time their dad threw a plate at his head. 'You were really naughty, Santosh,' my mother said. 'You never listened to me and would do whatever you wanted to do.' She smiled, and my father laughed.

I felt something inside me light up. I leaned forwards. 'Dad, I'm sorry.' He looked confusedly at me and then at my mother. 'I'm sorry. That day when I said that I didn't need your help, that I could figure it out myself, I was wrong. I'm sorry for being so arrogant. I shouldn't have said it. You didn't deserve that from me. You've done so much for me, and I know you were just trying to protect me. I'm also sorry for leaving India, leaving you. I know you needed me, but I was too consumed in myself to know any better. I shouldn't have argued with you; you had every right to question me, but I just pushed you away.' Tears spilled from my eyes as I continued letting all my burdens out. I leaned towards my father's feet as I had done all those years ago. In Indian culture, touching a person's feet signals that you respect them. The gesture symbolises that you are willing to bow down and surrender to their age, wisdom and spirituality to seek forgiveness. In return, the elder generally places their hands on top of your head, blessing you.

'Dad, I'm sorry for everything. Please forgive me and I'm so grateful for everything you've done for me. I love you.'

My father stood up, raising me with him. He hugged me, holding me close. 'I know,' he said gently. With that, we walked into the house for dinner. As we entered the hallway, my father turned towards me. He paused and looked at me meaningfully. 'You've asked for our forgiveness, however, have you forgiven yourself?'

I froze, taken aback by his words. I had realised my mistakes and asked for forgiveness from everyone I had hurt. But had I forgiven myself?

Through my self-discovery, I had come face to face with all my own conditioned behaviours and debilitating emotions. Initially I had been ashamed of them, hating the person that I used to be. However, now I accepted who I was, and the person I had become. I accepted all the bad and the good, and in the process, I had granted myself the greatest self-respect and love—forgiveness.

*   *   *

Less than a year later, my father passed away. His death was sudden, and I didn't have the opportunity to see him before he passed. I am eternally grateful to have been given the opportunity to learn this last lesson on forgiveness from him, and to have let him know how much I loved him before it was too late.

Twenty-three

The Sun of Tomorrow

Simple acts of kindness light the path ahead and lead to a more peaceful existence.

Being back home, I couldn't help but think about Abdul, who had fed me and given me a bed for the night after the lecture I'd attended with Mads and his father. It had been years since I'd been back to my original home and I was glad that my parents had moved back to the picturesque village when my father retired. The blue sky dotted with fluffy clouds persuaded me that a long walk through my hometown was a perfect way to spend the day.

After having breakfast and packing my backpack with bottles of water and snacks, I made my way through the village. Although for the first time in years I felt comfortable and happy, I still yearned to be a young boy, racing through the green paddy fields with my friends with not a care in the world and assurance that the sun would rise again in the morning so that we could play.

When I reached the green clearing where we used to play, I

looked for the big mango tree. It was gone. Many of the coconut trees that lined the fields, creating a beautiful backdrop against the blue sky, were also gone. The lush, tall grass found in the paddy fields seemed to have perished, leaving muddy pools of water littered with plastic rubbish. As I walked on, I noticed that the neighbouring fields had disappeared, replaced by the tall concrete buildings. The birds that used to dart from the trees, flying freely in the sky, had vanished, as if terrified by the tall, block monsters.

Walking further, I saw construction sites where scaffolding on the massive apartment blocks dominated the sky. Plastic and construction materials littered the ground, some flying around in the breeze and travelling into the distance. The tree-lined streets were replaced by tar roads; the picturesque village had lost its beautiful greenery. People had left the village in search of jobs and success in neighbouring, bustling cities. My friends, the families that lived around us, had disappeared. The village that I remembered had gone. Only my memory of its tranquillity, the few quaint homes and the narrow streets remained.

Saddened by how much had changed, I continued walking past the village on the main road towards the next village. The roads were tarred, and cars and buses noisily rushed past. I wondered if I should have borrowed my father's car, but it was too late. Although so much had changed, I could still make out homes and agricultural fields that had lasted the test of time and withstood corporations. Many rice and vegetable fields had been bought by greedy corporations who wanted to build apartments or resorts. However, in between the building sites, there were always a few remaining fields, lush with grass and growth, where cows grazed and wild rabbits skipped through the long grass. The pure smell of earth and rain was still strong over the stench of pollution and concrete. The sun rose higher into the sky, reaching its peak.

Sweating through my cotton shirt, I realised that I had underestimated India's heat. The sun glared down upon the land, while the tropics' humidity made the heat even more unbearable. It was at this moment that I wished I could find a mango tree. I would've had a snack of the fruit, and the long branches would have been the perfect place to rest from the sun. Smiling, I walked on, knowing that those days were now memories. Most of the fruit trees had been cut down to make way for the road. I walked for another hour until I caught sight of a familiar gate. It wasn't until I neared the wooden gate that I thought about how foolish this was. Abdul might not even live here anymore. He wouldn't even recognise me if he did. But, as these thoughts flooded my head, I observed them and became aware and conscious of the mind noise in my head, a practice which I had been following, to bring me back to the present.

With that clarity, I pulled on the bell hanging from the pillar of the gate. It let out a loud ping as I waited. No one answered, so I continued to wait. I considered going to the village to ask someone when I heard a little giggle above me. I looked up in surprise, looking for the source of the noise in the wide, branching tree that shaded the entire house. Squinting, I noticed a grinning face with shining mischievous eyes. 'Hello, is anyone there?' I called out. The child went silent, and I smiled as I saw slight movement between the branches. 'I know you're there.'

Acquiescing, the kid jumped from the tall branch of the tree, landing perfectly on his two feet. I smiled, remembering when I could do that as well. He looked up at me with the same curious yet mischievous eyes while I looked around for his parents. 'Hello, I'm looking for Abdul. He used to live here.'

The boy looked at me curiously, taking in my clothes, linen pants, and the backpack hanging on my shoulder. 'He's out in the field,' he replied cautiously. I smiled as he grinned back, as if realising that I am no threat. This kid was street smart. I recognised it because most children who live in villages are.

'I'm an old friend of Abdul—Santosh—and I was hoping to see him. Could you tell me where the field is?'

'I can take you,' the boy said. 'It's not far.' I stepped back from the gate, indicating that I was willing to follow him. He smiled, liking the fact that an adult was listening and following him. He skipped ahead of me, slowing down when I was too slow.

As we neared the town he waved and called out to some of the people he saw around. I was surprised when we walked past the old tea shop. The same shop that I had been to countless times as a kid. The boy stopped in front of it, quickly chatting to an elderly man with a beard and a white dhoti. They looked over at me, so I walked faster to catch up to the boy. 'Santosh! My boy, you've grown up.' The elderly man looked at me fondly as I smiled, recognising the owner of the tea store.

'Unni uncle, wow, you've kept the shop the same as always.'

He nodded proudly. 'Your father told me you were coming back to visit. I saw him at a wedding last month.'

I smiled. News travelled fast in such a small town, even between neighbouring towns.

'Unni uncle, I'm looking for Abdul. Is he here?'

Unni uncle nodded, 'He's in the fields. The crops aren't doing too well this year. Not enough rain.'

I nodded and followed as the boy continued to skip towards the fields. 'I'll come back here soon. I'm not leaving without having some of your specialty chai and vadai,' I called out to him. Unni uncle laughed and waved as he went into the shade of his store.

When we finally reached the fields, I couldn't help but stop in awe. It was so beautiful. Abundant and green. The paddy fields were thriving with narrow canals of water flowing between the fields. Men and women wearing woven, wide-brimmed hats were scattered around the vast fields, working away at the crop and tending to the new seedlings. The little boy skipped ahead, forcing me to speed up and follow him. He balanced on the mud ridge, which served as a track for anyone not wanting to wade into the water. I followed, making sure to tread carefully and not slip into the mud and water below. I rolled my eyes as the boy raced across and waited for me on the other side. He grinned cunningly.

'What's your name?' I asked him.

'Gopal,' he answered.

'How do you know Abdul?' I asked curiously.

179

Ignoring my question, he pointed out someone in the distance. I looked up to where he was pointing to see the familiar figure of Abdul. I carefully walked towards him while the boy bounded ahead, alerting him of our arrival.

By the time I reached them, the boy and Abdul were in deep conversation. I presume the boy was telling him that I had come to see him. He looked at me perplexed for a moment, then a jolt of recognition flashed through his eyes, and his face relaxed into a smile. 'Santosh! What a surprise.'

I grinned at how easily he remembered and recognised me. It had been thirty years since I last saw him, and he still recognised me. Abdul had aged, deep wrinkles lining his face from hours in the brutal sun.

'I brought him to you,' said the boy. 'He said he's an old friend.'

Abdul looked down at him sternly. 'Gopal, I thought you were sick. Sick enough that you couldn't go to school. But instead, you're traipsing across the whole village with boundless energy.' The boy was smart enough to look sheepish, and I smiled as he looked towards me guiltily.

'It's my fault, Abdul,' I said. 'I asked him to show me the way to find you.' I ignored the hopeful look the boy sent my way. Patting him on the back, I smiled down at him as he beamed at me gratefully. He reminded me of my younger self.

Abdul laughed, not buying a word of what I said, but he didn't say anything. 'Come, let's go. I've had enough for today.' He collected his tools and herded us towards the village centre. Gopal ran ahead, waving at other village boys and enjoying the freedom of youth. Meanwhile, Abdul and I casually meandered across the field while he asked about my vacation.

When we reached Unni uncle's store, we stopped, and Abdul led us inside. Gopal ran off to school as the bell rang throughout the village, signalling the school day's end. At the sound of the bell, Abdul looked up, remembering something. 'Santosh, give me one minute; I have something to do at school. I'll be back very soon. Please, continue without me,' he said as the chai and snacks were placed on our table.

'Oh ... sure, no problem. I'll be here.'

As Abdul left, Unni uncle came and sat opposite me, watching as Abdul walked towards the school. 'That man. He never stops. Never.' Unni uncle shook his head.

Sensing something interesting, I leaned towards him, taking a sip of the warm, sweet chai. 'What do you mean?' I asked curiously. As much as I appreciated Abdul's presence, I hardly knew the man.

'Oh, Abdul is just so invested in the school, in his farming, in the village and most of all his children. He'll do anything for his children and for this town. Even give up his own life.' I listened, not wanting to interrupt Unni uncle's flow. He looked at me, seeing the confusion on my face. 'Abdul has lived in this village ever since he was a young child. His parents lived in the same house—his father was a farmer; his mother was a teacher who became a housewife to take care of her family. Abdul had been a smart boy. Highly intelligent. His father put him in the state-run school, which is an hour away, and his mother tutored him. It was expensive, the travel every day, not to mention tedious for young Abdul. Abdul's father had been very invested in his son's education. He wanted him to become an engineer, to go overseas.'

Unni uncle's deep voice rumbled on as he went back into his memories. 'Abdul did very well in school, ranked first in the state in his tenth-grade exams. We were all so proud of him. He was the town's glory. Every mother in the town loved him and every father was proud of him. When he finished his year twelve, Abdul got a scholarship to study in a big university in America. His father was so proud. His son was finally achieving his dream. Abdul was excited as well and on the day he left, the whole district bid him farewell. He was a good boy. He wrote home every week, his father reading out his letters to everyone who would listen. Everyone wanted to know how he was doing. He was a son to everyone here. The years went on and Abdul finished college and got a job as an engineer in the States. His father was overjoyed. However, just weeks after accepting his new job, Abdul's mother was taken ill. We were all there to help her and she was getting better. However, for some reason, she became extremely ill very suddenly. His father tried to hide the information, not wanting his son to worry. But Abdul's mother wanted to see her son. She wanted to see him before she died. Eventually, we all persuaded his father to call Abdul, but he was stubborn. Finally, when it became serious, I called Abdul. His father was furious, but I knew that it was the right thing. Abdul came back home immediately. He was a good boy, so he dropped everything and came back. His job was on hold, as the people at his work in the US were considerate. When Abdul came home, he immediately took his mother to a hospital. Back in those days, hospitals were expensive and extremely hard to reach. He hired a car and took her to the nearest hospital in the city. However, when he got there, he realised that he needed to take his mother to Bombay. They needed some new technology or machine to help her, so he flew her to Bombay. Abdul's father had to stay here to take care of the farm, but his son took care of everything. Soon, Abdul's mother was well and came back home. But something had changed for Abdul.

'When they returned, Abdul spent a lot of time taking care of his mother, helping his father and spending time here in the village. He stayed for a couple of weeks and we didn't really question it. He was making sure his mother was fine.

'Then one day Abdul's father came to the shop crestfallen and told me that his son had quit his job in the US and was going to stay in India. Abdul's father was shattered. We all were. All that potential. All that hope. Abdul had let us all down.'

I listened to Unni uncle keenly.

'Abdul had his own plans. Plans bigger than us, bigger than his father's plans. It took us years to finally understand that. After his mother got better, he left for Bombay. We don't know what he did there, but he always came to visit. It was there that he met Ananya, his wife. She was beautiful in all the ways that mattered. She had a beautiful heart, and his parents loved her. They didn't stay here for long, but they always visited. When she died, he took it hard. We all did. She was incredibly young ... so was he.'

Unni uncle stopped and looked up towards the sky, in memory, in respect. Then he kept going. He was an amazing storyteller, pulling you into his mind, making you see what he saw.

'As Abdul's parents got older, he returned to the village. His mother passed first. Peacefully, with her son and husband beside her. She was happy. His father got older, so Abdul would go into the fields for him. He worked hard. Always has done. The lands and crops flourished under his care, and he loved it. His father passed a few years later, and Abdul cared for him until the last moment. The ever-patient, ever-loving son. During those last days, I don't think Abdul's father could have been any prouder of his son, even if he had been the richest man in the world. Abdul's father told me one night before he died, "He's kind, hard-working and brave. What more could I ask for in a son?"'

My heart felt heavy as I listened.

'After his parents' death, the house grew lonely. But not for long ... Sharadha, one of the women who worked in the fields, fell extremely sick one day. Abdul, being so considerate, had taken her to the hospital, but it had been too late. She died from some congenital disease. She left behind a five-year-old son. Young, mischievous, vulnerable, and orphaned—but Abdul took him in. His name was Amit. He looked after him as his own son. Raised him. Soon there were a couple more children under Abdul's wing. We didn't know where they were from, but they were happy. A family. The quiet house became alive with the laughter and love of the children.'

I remembered back to the young boy and the girls I had met

when I was a child. Where were they now? Amit, the young boy who gave me the glass of water when I visited Abdul's home for the first time, where is he? I was about to ask when Unni uncle paused. Looking up at the approaching Abdul, followed by two boys, Gopal, and another smaller boy. They were deep in animated conversation. 'Santosh, do you mind if we go home?' he said. 'The children will be home, and I need to be there. We can talk together there.'

Nodding, I stood up, saying a heartfelt goodbye to Unni uncle. 'Next time come back with the family,' he said as I left, and I promised that I would.

We walked back to Abdul's humble home as the boys continued arguing and discussing something important. Abdul and I followed them. He asked me about my family, my parents. I answered earnestly, telling him about my life in Australia and my job. I told him about my kids and he smiled, asking how old they were. When we finally reached the gate, Abdul walked in, leading me to the same open patio in the front with the jute chairs. I sat down while he went inside with the boys. The home was as tranquil as I remembered. Lovely, lush, broad trees protected the house from the heat of the sun. The weeping willow tree draped its leaves over the garden, creating a perfect hiding place for children. Birds chittered in the wide trees surrounding the house and the sound of a cow mooing echoed in the distance. I closed my eyes and breathed in the fresh, green air as I sat in the house's shadow.

*   *   *

Abdul and I sat on that patio and talked for hours. We talked about everything and nothing. His five children came outside and he introduced them all to me, including cheeky Gopal. They were kind, intelligent, and full of life—all five of them taking care of one another and driving each other crazy. There was a tender moment, as the sun drifted lower in the sky, when the children sat outside in the garden reading and completing their homework together—books, pencils, and children sprawled across the grass, each child in their own world, yet together. The oldest looked out for the younger ones, being stern yet kind as she helped them with their work with maternal grace. She was hardly thirteen, yet so mature and grounded. They asked me many questions about Australia, my home, my kids, my age. They were curious, childish, and Abdul just let them be themselves. He listened to them with the utmost patience, leaning down or kneeling to their level when they talked. He made them feel heard. He let them embrace their childhood and raised them with love. As darkness curled in the periphery of the garden, giving way to evening, Abdul and I sat in silence, aware of the world around us, the soft whispers of noise in the distance, the children laughing and arguing inside. We sat there together, just being.

'What happened? What changed?' I asked tentatively.

Abdul didn't even question what I was asking. He already knew. He knew I was alluding to the change that transformed his life. Made him leave his job in the US and settle in a secluded, humble village in India.

He smiled. 'It was so long ago, yet it seems like just last

week. Well, I'm guessing Unni already told you the story. I had finished my degree at Columbia and had accepted a position at a multinational company in the US. I should've been happy. I guess I told myself that I was happy, but I ... I felt lost ... incomplete. Twenty-five years old, about to fulfil all my dreams, and I felt incomplete. When I got accepted to Columbia, my father had been so proud. He was even prouder when I got my job. It was everything he had dreamed of, for him, for me. I had worked very hard since I was young, to do well in life, to be successful, to make him proud, to make my village proud. But there was always something inside me ... something that yearned for something else. The American dream for success, money, happiness wasn't my dream. It was my father's dream, and soon it had become mine. I guess I hoped that if I reached it, I would feel complete. My education was the most important part of this dream.

'My mother, being a teacher, had taught me everything I knew. She taught everyone; our house used to be full of children coming to learn. She taught every child their first letters, their first words. She was the one who initiated and started the first school in this village. Until that point, the nearest school had been several kilometres away in the neighbouring village. My father was in awe of her and her passion for teaching. So was I. She was the best teacher anyone could ask for. She taught with kindness and commitment and every word she conveyed would fall perfectly into the child's mind. She was an incredible woman. When she fell ill, I realised that my father had tried to hide the severity of her illness from me. He meant well, but I was really

187

angry. Angry that he thought my job was more important than my mother. Furious that he thought I valued my position at the company more than my mother. When Unni called me telling me how sick she was, I immediately dropped everything and came home. The company was considerate and gave me some time.

'When I came back, I knew she wasn't well. She needed immediate medical help. Back then, there were no hospitals nearby and when we went to the hospital in the city, they weren't equipped for the specialised care that she needed. So, I took her to Bombay where she could get specialised help. It was there that I realised there was much more to life than I'd previously thought. I'd had an epiphany, of sorts. It was an afternoon, I don't remember the day or time, but I was at the counter for medication when an ambulance siren rang at the emergency entrance. Doctors and nurses rushed past, wheeling a stretcher between them. A small boy lay unconscious across the stretcher. Blood poured thick and red from a wound on his head, very bright against the stark, white linen. He looked so small, so vulnerable, on that stretcher, his frame barely taking up half of the space. The medics rushed towards the emergency rooms with the boy between them. When I turned towards the woman at the counter, she gave me the slip and told me to wait. I waited among others for the medication. A doctor then came out of the emergency room, looking hurried and stressed. "Is there anyone here, with the boy?" the doctor said. "Family of the young boy?"

'The room went silent. I looked around, hoping that his family may be there, but there was no one. When my number was called,

I walked towards the counter, collected my medicines and was about to make my way to my mother's private room. That's when the doctor walked out with a nurse. "Doctor, no one has come to claim him. There are no relatives. The driver who hit the boy took off and the person who called the ambulance has long gone. It seems the boy is a street child and has no one."

'The doctor ran his hand through his hair, evidently thinking. "How can we do the procedure, doctor?" the nurse asked. "He has no guardian, no money to pay."

'"We will have to transfer him to a government hospital," the doctor stated. "We cannot do the procedure here. Unfortunately, those are the rules. But I don't know if he'll make it. The injury is severe, and the subdural hematoma is putting pressure on his brain."

'I listened in shock, realising the implications. That boy could die. This instant, with no-one to save him. I heard myself calling out before my brain processed what I was doing. "Doctor, please, save the boy. I'll pay his medical bill. Just save the boy."

'The doctor replied, "But you're not his family, not his guardian."

'I felt desperate about his situation and couldn't understand why the doctor was still standing there. "I don't care," I said. "He is alone, maybe even orphaned, so he is a child of the state, and I will fund his medical expenses. Please." The doctor still hesitated, staring at me. "You said his injuries are life-threatening," I continued. "Please save him." With that, he nodded and walked into the emergency room. To save a life, I hoped.

'I stood there, unsure what to do next as the nurse left. Within moments, another nurse took her place, asking me to sign forms and pay the initial fee. I obliged, my mind dazed and confused. All I cared about was that child. He needed to be okay. The surgery went for hours. As far as I knew, it had been days. I went to see my mother, but she was still unconscious from the drugs. So I waited downstairs near the emergency room, alternating between my mother's and the child's rooms every few hours.

'When the doctor finally came out, I stood up, studying him, trying to look into his eyes. He nodded, smiling. The child was alright. "He's stable," the doctor said, "We need to watch him for the next forty-eight hours. He'll be transferred soon." The doctor looked at me with relief in his eyes. Rules and guidelines were going to kill that child and the doctor had been shackled by them, but I had given him an option to save the child. For that, he was grateful. I smiled, acknowledging his skill in saving the boy, and then sat down to wait. We didn't need forty-eight hours. The child was awake in twenty-four. I was sitting beside him, slumped back over the chair, sleeping. I had been startled awake by a young child groaning. I got up as the boy opened his eyes and took in his surroundings. His eyes widened, filled with fear and confusion. He looked down at his arm, at the needles puncturing his stick-like limbs. Tears rolled down his cheeks.

'I walked over tentatively, not wanting to scare him. "It's okay," I said. "You're okay. Don't be scared. My name is Abdul. You're in a hospital. You had a bit of a fall, so the doctors had to take care of you." His eyes widened as he looked around. "They fixed you all up, but they just want you to stay so you can get better, stronger." I smiled at him, encouraging him to relax in my presence. He seemed to sense that I wasn't dangerous, as I saw him visibly deflate and resign himself to the situation. I could tell that he was intelligent. His eyes shone with instinct—no wonder he survived alone for so long. He was street smart, led by intuition. "I'll be right back, okay. I'm just going to call the doctor." He nodded, his eyes drooping with fatigue. Poor kid, he didn't deserve this.

'I followed the doctor as he examined the child, peering over his charts. He tested his reflexes and made sure that the boy had no neurological deficits. He seemed fine, just recovering. Throughout the whole process, the boy didn't say anything. When the doctor asked him his name, he stayed silent. Over the next few days, I alternated between tending to my recovering mother and the young boy. Over time he warmed to me. He didn't know his real name, but apparently, people called him "Chottu". He also didn't know how old he was, but the doctor assumed that he was around seven years old. Chottu was a curious little kid. When he started to feel better, the doctor recommended that he walk a bit. I took him on strolls throughout the wards, where he would pop his head into every room. Sometimes, when I got back from seeing my mother, he would have disappeared, and I would find him sitting with the nurses, asking them many questions. Everyone liked the young child; his innocent curiosity and joy were heartwarming. No matter what he had been through, it hadn't hardened him yet.

'I took him to see my mother one day, holding his hand as he walked through the new block; a ward at the hospital yet to be discovered. My mother was sitting up, reading a book in her lap. As we entered, she beamed at the little boy, who shared his toothy grin. She called him over and lifted him into her lap. I almost called out to stop her, but she lifted him with ease even though she was recovering from her illness. He was too skinny, I thought. She thought so too. I watched her studying his tiny wrists and thin arms. "So, this is little Chottu," she said. "My son tells me that you're a mischievous one." She tickled him, and he giggled while squirming in her arms. I went out to get some food, and when I returned, Chottu was lying beside my mother, listening as she read from her book. He had no idea what she was saying, but her words put him into a trance. I smiled, remembering when she used to read to me as a kid. Her soft, clear voice rang like a little bell. She was amazing with kids.

'As my mother and Chottu got better, I realised that we would have to go home. My father called every day and my mother missed him. As soon as the doctor gave the word, we would be on a flight back to Kerala. But, as the days continued and my mother recovered, I couldn't help but think of young Chottu. I couldn't leave him abandoned in this hospital. He needed to be somewhere safe.

'On the day that Chottu was discharged, I decided that he wouldn't be left on the streets again. I had talked to the doctor, police and the authorities. He had no kin, no guardian, no home. Taking Chottu's hand, I explained to him that he was going to a home. A big home, where he would have plenty of friends, brothers, and sisters. He would be safe and wouldn't have to live alone on the streets again. He seemed hesitant and I saw the conflict in his eyes as he left the hospital and headed to the car. This place was safe, and he felt at home. He didn't want to leave, especially since he'd made many friends at the hospital and was blossoming from the much-needed love he received.

'When we finally arrived at the home after an hour of travel, a kind nun stood at the entrance. The beautiful brick house was surrounded by trees, nature and children playing in the playground. The nun walked over, introduced herself and then bent down to talk to Chottu. He seemed hesitant, scared, but he gave her a pleasant smile. She called some children over—two girls and a young boy. They smiled at us. "Chottu, why don't you go play with them," she said kindly. He looked up at me, pleading with me not to go.

'"Chottu, go on!" I said. "Go play."

'He reluctantly went off with the children, as the nun showed me around the home. "Too many children are abandoned. Left to fend for themselves. Many of them don't make it. The world can be a scary place, especially when they are so vulnerable. But I always believe that God will look after his children, as he has with Chottu. He will be well cared for here." I turned to look towards Chottu, smiling as he twirled a skipping rope with his new friends. He would be well cared for here. So, I had to say goodbye. I had to leave him. At least he was in a safer place.

'When we arrived back home, it was all I could think

about—the millions of lost and abandoned children who were alone. So many children with no one to care for them. So many young lives at risk. I couldn't shake the sadness, despair and anger from my mind. Why was no one looking out for them? Why didn't the state care about its children? For weeks, it had been all that I could think about. Chottu. Bleeding and alone. The children at the home—happy, safe, loved. In that moment, I realised that if no one would look after those children, then I would. At least some of them. I knew then with complete clarity what I needed to do. What was my purpose in life? I knew then. And there was no turning back ...'

I paused, not daring to move as Abdul swept through his memory, his eyes clouded in recollection.

'I quit my job in the US and told my parents. When I told my mother, she had looked at me with so much pride, love and gratitude. "I always knew you were special," she said. "From the moment you first smiled, I knew you were here to shed light on the world." My father was less enthused. He couldn't understand why I would give up my dream, rather his dream. It was everything I had ever wanted. Yet it wasn't. My dream had changed. When my mother finally got better, I headed back to Bombay. I volunteered at the care home for a few months, learning and being with the children. It was then that I developed ideas to help children who were alone, abandoned and struggling. I began by starting another care home for children, giving them a safe, happy sanctuary, away from the hardship of the streets and the city. I continued defending children for years and that's how I met my wife. She was a teacher who loved children. She was so passionate and so full of awe for her children. Together we continued our vision.

'When she passed, I felt so lost. I didn't know what to do. But the children helped me come back. I knew I had to find a way back for them, so I could help them. I knew that was what she would've wanted me to do. As the years went by, my parents grew old. When my mother's health deteriorated, I went back home. My aging parents needed me, so I decided to stay and support them. They had supported me throughout my whole life. It was finally my time to be there when they needed me most. I wasn't worried, though. I had enough people in Bombay who would continue to look out for the children. I tended to my mother until she passed and then helped my father as much as I could. He was a proud, determined man. I always admired that about him. Even into his late sixties, he would wake at the crack of dawn and tend to his field until sunset—a true farmer.

'Over time, I found myself drifting towards the fields, watching him, learning from him. Soon, I was in the middle of it, tending to the land with him. He taught me everything. As he became more and more tired, I took over. He came to supervise, sitting in the sun with Unni. It was then that I realised how much joy farming gave me. Taking care of the earth, watching seedlings sprout into plants, eating the crops that I grew, and feeding others with its energy and nutrients. Watching the energy that I put into the land turn into something tangible, something useful. It was fulfilling. Soon, my father became incredibly old, and he passed. I continued without him. And here I am, old, tired, but content ... content with my family,' he said, looking at his home with his children.

I took a deep breath, allowing myself to come back to the present. Watching as the farms in my mind drifted away from the story into the cool front yard of Abdul's home. The sun was dipping, shading the world in dusky orange, gold, and pink. Lights twinkled inside the house, illuminating Abdul's face. Wow. He had lived. Abdul had truly lived. That was one incredible story. I looked at my watch—half-past four. My father was coming to pick me up shortly. I stood up. 'Abdul, thank you! That was incredible. I appreciate you sharing that with me.'

Abdul stood up as a car arrived at the front of Abdul's house. My father had arrived. He smiled. 'Not a problem. Santosh, thank you for visiting me. It means a lot.' He gave me a loving, gentle hug. I walked to the car as Abdul opened the gate for me. 'Santosh!' Abdul called. 'Did you find the answer to that question?'

I paused and smiled. 'I think I did.'

He nodded at me, a glitter in his eyes. 'I knew you would.'

That evening I went to the beach near my village. A quiet, isolated beach the locals kept secret from tourists. Sitting on the rather lonely beach, I was immersed in the beauty and grace of the evening sun, just about to say goodbye for the day and fade slowly away. The golden sand was still a bit warm from the sun's generous warmth. The sea was, as usual, vibrant and full of energy.

It was magnificent to see the waves of different shapes and

sizes come up for a moment to embrace each other and disappear back into the sea, only to appear a moment later with a different shape to embrace and greet a new set of waves. This appeared to go on forever. They are part of the sea, yet they take on different shapes each time and go back into the sea to be part of it. *Unanimity and Oneness of epic proportions*, I thought to myself.

I suppose we human beings are similar to the waves of the sea. We are part of the whole. We take on different shapes, perhaps different colours, yet we are part of the whole, or rather, we make up the whole. The only difference is that our minds think that we are separated from each other by colour, race, shape, ideology, and religion, which create a mighty barrier leading to conflict, hatred, and violence. The story of the sea is an amazing story of being one with everything.

I thought about Abdul. About the question that remained unanswered: *Who am I? Who am I really?*

My name is Santosh. I need a name for my physical form. I need a passport so others can identify me and so I can function in society. Beyond that, does my name have any relevance? Maybe the challenge is that I have fully identified my name with my body, mind and baggage, which is fine at an intellectual level. However, to thrive and connect with the Universal Intelligence, I must go beyond my mind-conceived conditioned self and dis-identify from my body, my mind and my baggage. When that happens, when my mind surrenders ... I am one with space. I am one with everything.

The moment I realised this, my heart swelled with love. Because when you are one with everything, when you are connected to everyone, every being, every living thing, you are overwhelmed with love. True love. Unconditional love. A love in which there is only giving without expectations of anything in return. The invisible mind-conceived barrier has finally lifted allowing the inner grace—the true self—to shine through and embrace other beings. A feeling of Oneness. This is the answer to all questions. Love. The greatest power in the world. *Why is there so much suffering in the world? Why do humans hurt one another? Discriminate between each other?* Because we are consumed by the mind, by an idea of who we are. We separate ourselves from others. I am Santosh, you are—but when you become aware of that identity and the associated baggage, in other words, become aware of the 'mind-conceived conditioned self', you are finally united with the Intelligence and every being in the universe. And at that moment of complete acceptance, the only power that holds you is true, real, pure, unconditional love.

I wish I could convey this simple and profound truth to my grandmother. Unfortunately, she is long gone now. Even if she was alive, I would not have been able to convince her or break through the thick layers of her conditioned baggage which she may have acquired from her ancestors or during her own upbringing, especially her identification with a certain caste, religion or social status. These are the same identities which have created barriers among humans. However, I can be the circuit breaker. I can cease the ignorant and unfair conditioning inherited by each new generation. I can free my children from the social barriers that created division, violence and hurt. Therefore, I have a choice. I have a role to play. I can be the role model.

Abdul had always known the answer to my question. He knew it then, and he knew it with utmost clarity now. In fact, he had understood the purpose of his manifestation much earlier in life. He also dared to pursue this purpose, to divert from his original path to something entirely new, challenging and fulfilling. Abdul realised what unconditional love was a long time ago; it shines and lives through all orphaned children. He has certainly made a difference to the world in which we live. The children he shared love with will now go into the world bright with its power and share it with many others throughout their lives. I am sure that the small ripple that Abdul created is making a big impact in this world when the world today has so many who lack that selfless, unconditional love. The lamp that Abdul lit is shining through in various forms.

As the sun finally bid goodbye for the day, allowing darkness to descend rather rapidly on the beach, I realised that Abdul certainly touched many lives. He changed mine significantly.

*   *   *

Abdul's inspiration and clarity had a significant effect on me. For the first time, I knew what I needed to do. I may have known for a while; however, I finally dared to pursue the thing I yearned. That night when I got home, I called my wife, telling her everything I thought. Being the ever-patient and generous woman she was, she listened without judgement and gave me the freedom to do what I wanted. I knew she was worried, reluctant about the big change that was going to ensue. But she also had faith that we would figure it all out, that somehow, we would be okay. That night, in the coolness of the Kannur breeze, I drafted an email. An email that would change my life and completely shatter the stability for which I had worked and strived. I wrote to the board members and requested them to start looking for a new CEO as I was resigning from the Biotech company in Melbourne, with six months' notice for them to transition. I couldn't keep working for a company. I couldn't keep rushing through my life, fulfilling other people's wishes. I needed to find my own feet. My own independence. My passion. When I finally sent the message, I felt a wave of calm drift over me, settling the fire of uncertainty that raged inside me. This was the right thing to do. It felt right. I had a sense of clarity in what I wanted to do. It had always been there, whispering inside me. Now I could finally hear it clearly, calling out to me. I didn't know what would happen next, but I had an idea and hope for the future.

*   *   *

I resigned from corporate life and started my own Biotech company from scratch in 2012. This provided me with a flexible lifestyle, time, and space to do what I really wanted. It wasn't without its challenges, but I could bring my practise of the 'art of conscious balance' to bring about 'presence' into what I was doing, and the connection to the Intelligence kept me grounded.

It was as if there was energy guiding me and looking after me at every step. This is what had been missing for so many years. It certainly took considerable attention, awareness and inner reflection to realise the extent of my own ignorance. I felt complete and content for the first time. I realised I was able to bring presence to everything. Even the mundane jobs, like chasing up payments from customers and packing up products to dispatch, became less of a hassle when I did so.

I also realised something else during this time—I needed to share this simple truth of life with anyone ready and willing to listen. To convey to them that liberation from the mind-conceived conditioned 'self' is possible. We don't have to go through intense suffering to free ourselves from that trap, but it's time to awaken. The sooner you do it, the better it is for you. If only our children knew about this secret earlier in life, they wouldn't have to go through the struggle and suffering that I have gone through. They could be liberated much sooner and be free to flourish, thrive and flower fully in life. The alternate form of liberation is death. Death ultimately liberates all of us from that trap once and for all. But that will be too late and futile. People should have a choice. They should be able to choose, to know that there is an alternative way to live—a life of joy, contentment, and love. I chose this life. I chose love.

Is this what Tom meant when he asked me to find the purpose in my life?

*   *   *

I woke up the next morning on my last day in India. It was a beautiful day, the sun shining through my open window, streaming throughout the house. I decided to go for a walk and find my special place. A place that had always been dear to my heart.

As I waded through the green paddy fields, my eyes fell upon an old Kerala-style house. What caught my attention was the elderly lady sitting on a wooden chair, staring blankly at the last remaining coconut trees around her house, as if in a silent conversation with them. It didn't require a second look at her face for me to fathom her deep sadness. Her wrinkled forehead and long-drawn eyes suggested that she had seen several decades of happiness and sadness. When she turned to look at me, it sent a chill down my spine. She looked at me with her unseeing eyes; an expression of disdain and disappointment. Like I was responsible for her sadness, responsible for robbing her of whatever she was missing. Perhaps I was. The society that we live in today seems callous and ruthless in the name of survival, filled with hatred, fear, ego, anger and selfishness. The joy, love and compassion seems to be edged out, once and for all. The self-centredness of my generation stripped her of her beautiful home. We deserted her and took away the beautiful natural world that had always been there for her. She was sad because we were making huge mistakes. Mistakes that would have dramatic repercussions for everyone's future. She saw us being ignorant and arrogant. We were not learning from our mistakes. We just kept repeating them. She was sad for us, the next generation, who would ruin the natural world. The natural world that had been home for humans for millennia.

A significant connection occurred between the elderly lady and me during that moment, although not a word or gesture was exchanged. She made me realise that there are thousands, if not millions, like her, all around the world. People who have been living with deep sadness and suffering. No one to notice them, and no one to care.

Before we parted ways, she gave me a gentle smile through her swollen eyes, as if to say to me that hope, joy, love, benevolence, and compassion will soon prevail. With that hope, I continued along, aware of the shift within me. That day I noticed the sorrow in another human being. Previously I'd failed to see it as I had been preoccupied with my own problems—a glimpse of the shift from my mind conceived conditioned 'self'? Maybe. I don't know.

*   *   *

I continued my trek past all my favourite childhood memories, but there was one place that I had to see. I was worried about what I would see when I got there because I didn't trust that it would still be there. So much had changed. There was no way it could still be there. As I walked around a familiar bend and past all the construction sites towards the village's furthest border, I saw it. Its angled surfaces were as familiar to me as the honeyed voice of an old friend—my broken hill. I laughed to myself in amazement, so relieved by its presence. I felt like I was eight years old again—free, rampant and happy. Looking up at it, I realised that it wasn't as tall as I remembered, and I climbed its rocky surface to get to my favourite place. The climb was much easier with my long legs and a better sense of balance. Eventually, when I reached the top, I turned to look at the view. The thriving green fields were replaced by cement foundations and littered with construction rubbish. The tall trees that stood guard around the village were gone and replaced by tar roads that led into the distance. Small clusters of children ran in between the roads, dodging the scaffolding of the high-rise buildings.

Forty-odd years later and it was still the same place, yet so much had changed. This is still the same land; the same mountains in the distance, the same broken hill, but so much was changing. Changing, because people are becoming more self-centred? I don't know. I stood over the crest of the hill just as I had done all those years ago.

Now as I stood on top of the hill, the same sun was dipping slowly down the sky. I turned to go back, aware of how long it had been since I'd last visited the broken hill. As I turned, I noticed it. A yellow flower. Not the same flower, yet it was identical in appearance. Bright, flourishing petals attached to a slim stem that reached out, straining to reach the sky. The only difference was that the tiny plant that sprouted on the crest of the hill had now grown and become a huge, wild bush covered in many similar flowers, almost like yellow specks of light that dotted the flourishing bush. Remembering my little yellow friend, I smiled. This tree and the hill stood as silent witness to the transformation that occurred throughout the years. Silently watching as people came and departed, as children played and grew up, it sat above the valley like a witness, just observing, accepting, embracing every change that came its way: rains, floods, brutal heat and even the heavy step of callous humans. Despite everything, this plant thrived.

I descended the steep slope carefully. Aware of the slipping rays of light. Aware that even the yellow flower, the tree and the broken hill, will perish one day. All 'things' will perish except for the 'nothingness'—the space. That space is who I am. The space remains eternal like a silent witness. I hurried back to the road to return to my car, but not before taking a final look.

The sun was taking a last peek before leaving for the day, leaving a faint glimmer of gold along the horizon. The darkness of night was beginning to envelop everything even though the sky was still bathed in swathes of pink and orange. And there among the beautiful watercolour backdrop was the perfect carved shape of my broken hill, crowned by the curling branches of the mighty tree, with specks of yellow-gold petals that shone against the dying rays of light.

In that moment I had a profound realisation. This beautiful flower that had withstood the destruction caused by humans, and still continued to spread joy and love, was the symbol of true unconditional love. Gifting the world its life, beauty, fragrance and energy, the flower expected nothing in return. I smiled at the miracle and beauty of nature. Despite being born from nature, humans are so different. We struggle to connect to the

Intelligence, and we live within a conditioned world. Perhaps this is what differentiates us from nature—our access to both the conditioned mind (intellect) and the Universal Intelligence. Our conditioned knowledge and mind have certainly helped the advancement of humanity, but at what cost? As our environment deteriorates around us, I realise that our biggest mistake is our lack of balance. Despite having both the intellect and Intelligence at our disposal, we have neglected to connect with the Universal Intelligence. Perhaps, if we had connected with the Intelligence, we would be living in an entirely different world.

Now, within the confines of our constructed society, the only way forward is to use both the intellect and the Intelligence in conscious balance. We need both.

This is possible with conscious awareness.

We need our mind (intellect) to help us survive within conditioned society, and the Intelligence to guide us towards a more sustainable, meaningful and joyous future. Thus, the 'Art of Conscious Balance' becomes inherently necessary in our lives. With harmonious balance between our intellect and the Universal Intelligence, we will have greater control over the lives we choose to lead and the future that we lead humanity towards.

I stared at the hill with my newfound understanding. And there, at the very crest of the hill, stood a single proud flower. It bowed its elegant head, acknowledging the truth of my understanding, as the last shaft of light illuminated its petals.

The touch of Truth

*The answers you search for never come when your mind
is busy. They come when your mind is quiet.*

W ithin our conditioned society, we are habituated to define
and understand things with our minds. Unfortunately,
we do the same when attempting to seek the Truth about
life. However, the Truth that we desperately seek cannot be
understood by the conditionings of the mind. When the mind
is in power, the Truth will remain elusive.

During my journey to the inner self, I realised that if you
desperately try to quiet the mind, it is like a dog chasing its own
tail. The most important thing is to find some peace and order in
life, and for our meaning-seeking mind to become silent . This
is a simple truth. But how can we do this?

When the mind that is constantly seeking becomes silent
(without any effort or intervention), it is in that silence the Truth
is revealed. In that moment of profound silence, all the answers
to our questions and challenges in life are revealed.

Human beings have achieved a great deal outwardly. We can go to the moon, explore space and revolutionise the world with technology. We have built massive civilisations and transformed modern life. But there is much to be learned from deep within. Unfortunately, in our race against life, the deeper, inner aspects of our lives elude us. When we finally take time to embrace our inner being, the hidden grace deep within us rises from the darkness and reveals the answers to our internal and external conflicts. Hence, the solution to all life's challenges is to awaken our profound, inner self. Once we achieve this, as a community we will become better, more conscious, connected, calm, creative, and compassionate beings. We will inevitably leave behind a better and healthier planet.

On a parting note, rather than desperately trying to seek (at the level of the mind) the Truth, if you are able to just observe and realise the interference of your own 'mind-conceived conditioning'—the same conditioning that prevents you from realising the Truth—you may be on a path that answers all the questions and challenges that pervade your life. This might even lead you to the absolute Truth. Don't trust me. Don't believe me. Embark on your own unique journey and discover the truth for yourself!

About the Author

Santosh Nambiar is the founder of the non-profit organisation Life a Meditation and Mindnoise Matters. Santosh is also registered as a mindfulness guide with the Meditation Association of Australia.

Santosh is the author of internationally acclaimed book *A New Way of Living*. His other book include, *In Between Thoughts, Intellect vs Intelligence* and *Taking Your Life from Mediocrity to Creativity*. His new book *The Art of Conscious Balance* takes a different route exploring his own personal pathway to clarity, peace, and purpose.

Santosh has a background in Molecular Biology and an MBA from Royal Melbourne Institute of Technology. He is the founder of a Biotech company based in Melbourne which provides support to universities in Australia and New Zealand towards biomedical research in finding a cure for diseases like cancer, cardiovascular diseases and ailments that threaten humanity's health.

Santosh lives in suburban Melbourne with his family of four.

When Santosh is not working on his new book, conducting mindfulness workshops, or charting a new course in his business, he is usually on his bike meandering the less-trodden regional areas of Victoria, taking in the breathtaking scenery of the little towns. He is also an avid fan of practical jokes, and enjoys watching countless YouTube videos of innocent people being pranked. He also likes pranking members of his own family at home.

www.santoshnambiar.com

CPSIA information can be obtained
at www.ICGtesting.com
Printed in the USA
LVHW050458020522
717671LV00027B/462

9 781925 707724